Dial Down the Drama

Dial Down the Drama

Reducing Conflict and Reconnecting with Your
Teenage Daughter—A Guide for Mothers Everywhere

COLLEEN O'GRADY

АMACOM

AMERICAN MANAGEMENT ASSOCIATION

New York • Atlanta • Brussels • Chicago • Mexico City • San Francisco
Shanghai • Tokyo • Toronto • Washington, D. C.

This publication is designed to provide accurate and authoritative information in regard to the subject matter covered. It is sold with the understanding that the publisher is not engaged in rendering legal, accounting, or other professional service. If legal advice or other expert assistance is required, the services of a competent professional person should be sought.

Library of Congress Cataloging-in-Publication Data
O'Grady, Colleen.
    Dial down the drama : reducing conflict and reconnecting with your teenage daughter? : a guide for mothers everywhere / Colleen O'Grady. — First Edition.
        pages cm
    Includes bibliographical references and index.
    ISBN 978-0-8144-3655-4 (paperback) — ISBN 978-0-8144-3656-1 (ebook)
1. Mothers and daughters. 2. Daughters—Psychology. 3. Interpersonal relations. 4. Parenting. I. Title.
    HQ755.85.O327 2015
    306.874'3—dc23   2015010326

About AMA
American Management Association (www.amanet.org) is a world leader in talent development, advancing the skills of individuals to drive business success. Our mission is to support the goals of individuals and organizations through a complete range of products and services, including classroom and virtual seminars, webcasts, webinars, podcasts, conferences, corporate and government solutions, business books, and research. AMA's approach to improving performance combines experiential learning— learning through doing—with opportunities for ongoing professional growth at every step of one's career journey.

Printing number
10 9 8 7 6 5 4 3 2 1

To my daughter, Erin,
My delight, who reminds me to live life to the fullest.

To my mom,
My rock, who has always encouraged me to be my best.

To my grandmother Nana,
My inspiration, who always told me "to thine own self be true."

Contents

PART III
Creating a New Future for You and Your Daughter

Acknowledgments

I want to give thanks . . .

To the many authentic and courageous moms who have opened their hearts and trusted me with their stories about their daughters over the past twenty-five years: It's because of you that I have written this book.

To my family: I am blessed to have such amazing parents: You have always believed in me even when I was an obstinate teenager; you always told me, "You could do anything you set your mind to." As it turned out, you were right. I don't know what I would do without *my sister, Cathy:* You have always had my back, and have been—and are—my constant cheerleader. And to *my dearest daughter, Erin:* You have been my greatest teacher. What a ride and journey your teenage years have been. I am grateful for being with you in the glory and the messiness, and watching you transform into a remarkable human being.

To my friends: I am grateful for all of you—Elizabeth, Glen, Jenny, Joan, Julia, Julie, Kevin, Kia, Lorna, Marie, Marty, Sherry, Teresa, and Tom. You have been there, listened, shared your stories, encouraged (even made me a few dinners), and prayed with me through the completion of this book.

To Christine Kane and the Platinum Mastermind: I'm eternally grateful for your fierce belief in my message; you had the foresight to say to me, "You know you need to write a book," and pierced my defenses. (Thus was this book conceived.) And many thanks to all my platinum friends who "got it" and celebrated each step of this journey with me. Especially Anna, Elaine, Jen, Starla , Stacey, and Sue, who have been there from the beginning.

To Christine Kloser and the Transformational Author Experience: You introduced me to everything I ever needed to know about writing a book, and you helped turn this passionate book novice into a published author.

To Jane Friou, my brilliant marketing coordinator: Thanks for your availability and honest critique when I needed another set of eyes, especially in the late night hours.

To Sara Arey and Ken Stone: You kept me centered and clear about who I am, my purpose, and how this book can serve the world.

To my wonderful agent Jacquie Flynn from Delbourgo Agency: You sent me an email that said "contact me if you haven't been snatched up." And so I did. I so appreciate your honesty, enthusiasm, energy, humor, and determination; you found my book the perfect home.

To the incredible team at AMACOM, especially my editor, Robert Nirkind: You patiently and strategically walked me through each chapter, and then turned me over to the tender ministrations of my copyeditor, Debbie Posner, who helped my manuscript shine.

Introduction

As I was finishing this book, I sat in a room with some very successful women entrepreneurs at a weekend retreat. These women were dressed in confidence as well as professional clothes. Then an interesting thing happened; the conversation switched from talking about their business to talking about being a mom. All these women happened to have teenage daughters. It didn't take long before the tears came. One mom talked about feeling guilty about not having enough time with her daughter. Another said, "I feel like a terrible mom sometimes because I can't handle my daughter's sassy and defiant attitude and I lose my temper." They talked about feeling like they weren't "good enough" moms. They admitted judging themselves constantly, questioning if they were good or bad moms, based on how their daughters were behaving. I was grateful for these women's honesty. Working moms as well as stay-at-home moms regularly think about how they are doing as moms and can be extremely hard on themselves. This is especially true for those with teenage daughters. Running a multimillion dollar business can feel like a piece of cake when facing a defiant and dramatic teenage daughter.

If you are reading this book, I know that you really care about your daughter and that you are tired and done with all the teenage drama.

Believe me, you're not the only one. With *Dial Down the Drama* we will raise the bar for what is possible for mother and daughter during the teenage years. You will learn to reduce conflict, reconnect with your teenage daughter, and reclaim your life.

Traditionally, parenting guides focus on techniques and scripts. But these books miss a key component in turning things around: Mom! You cannot be expected to always be completely detached and objective. When your daughter turns on you, or betrays your trust, it can break your heart or make you furious. When your daughter is out past curfew and doesn't return your text messages, you panic. You feel these things deeply because this is your child, your own flesh and blood. And you can take things personally. Add to this that you are already stressed enough, under tremendous pressure to do it all and to do it perfectly.

And, as a mom, you can strongly identify with your teenage daughter. What happens or doesn't happen to your daughter can bring up your own issues, regrets, and traumas. It's no wonder that your drama-filled daughter can turn you into a Drama Mama. The good news is that it doesn't have to be this way. This seemingly hopeless situation can be turned around.

How do I know this? I have worked with families, specifically mothers and daughters, for over twenty-five years as a licensed marriage and family therapist. I have supervised and trained clinicians in psychiatric hospitals and outpatient clinics. I have worked with mothers and daughters locally in my private practice, and with moms all over the world in my Power Your Parenting programs through my website.

But most important, I am a mom of a teenage daughter. I started writing this book when my daughter was a sophomore in high school, and I finished this manuscript when she was nineteen. There were times I thought I must be crazy for writing about the mother–daughter relationship when I was living it. I enjoy my life with my daughter. She is one of my favorite people on this planet. However, it hasn't always been that way. When she was an early teen I fell hook, line, and sinker into the drama. My academic theories melted away when my own daughter lashed out at me, and, to be honest, I reacted in kind, but with grown-up words.

Drama negatively impacts your relationship with your daughter and your parenting. It's hard for anyone to thrive in a drama-filled environment. Drama brings discouragement and resentment. It's easy to become jaded. It's easy to give up on having an enjoyable connection with your daughter. You're suddenly just hoping to make it through the day, and to survive the teenage years.

But that's not good enough. It's time to reclaim a good relationship with your daughter. Early adolescence starts at nine; you don't want to dread the next nine while your daughter still lives at home. It's time to raise your expectations and set new goals for what's possible during your daughter's teenage years. You'll find that when you dial down the drama, there is an upside to living with a teenage girl. Your daughter reminds you to laugh, to have fun, to chill, to put yourself out there, to try new things, to create adventure, and to live fully alive.

But the best part is that you can have an amazing authentic relationship with your daughter. This doesn't mean that you are her best friend. But you don't want to be her enemy, either. You can hold on to your authority as mom and still have a richly rewarding connection.

A healthy mother–daughter relationship is essential for parenting and vital for your daughter's well-being. The article "Adolescent-parent attachment: Bonds that support healthy development," by Marlene M. Moretti and Maya Peled, confirms that a healthy connection between a parent and teen is linked to better performance and coping strategies for both parties, and more competence in peer relationships. A healthy connection is correlated with fewer mental health problems such as anxiety, depression, conduct disorder, and aggression. Their research also indicated lower rates of teenage pregnancy, eating disorders, excessive drinking, drug use, and risky sexual behavior. Seems well worth the effort.

I'm not saying this is easy. There are many challenges to this mother–daughter connection. But *Dial Down the Drama* will guide you through the intricacies of the teenage years. You'll learn how to reduce conflict, redeem mistakes, and keep your relationship with your daughter intact, even in the hard times.

Central to the book is neuroscience, with a particular focus on what's different about the teenage brain. Understanding that teenagers have an undeveloped prefrontal cortex, which is what is responsible for planning ahead, managing emotions, self-awareness, and more, will help you understand her behavior, and can only benefit your relationship with your daughter. You will learn that stress, pressure, frustration, worry, anger, or exhaustion can send either you or your daughter straight to the stress response of fight, flight, or freeze. In these circumstances, the lower brain is in control. This is where much of the drama starts. Understanding the brain is also key to your ability to have successful conversations with your daughter. Throughout the book you will be given scripts and strategies to open communication with your daughter, create a daily connection, and work through tough issues. In addition, you will get practical steps, how-tos, and solutions to help you parent well, live healthy, and be your best.

How This Book Is Organized

This book is divided into three parts that build upon each other. In Part I, we'll focus on helping you to regain your perspective as a mom and, in the process, to regain your life as a woman. We begin by looking at some implicit cultural messages, such as "It's selfish to pay attention to me" and "Mothers are supposed to do it all and get everything right," that have deep impact on your parenting. I call them *Powerless* Parenting Messages because, in fact, they *dis*empower. These messages influence how you think and how you act. It's no surprise that with messages like these, you are left discouraged, stressed, and exhausted. This is turned around with some Powerful Parenting Messages that will give you a fresh perspective and a new clarity when dealing with your teenage daughter. These new messages also decrease the worry and the pressure, which will help you to feel like yourself again. They will also help you dismantle the worry and fear, triggered by your teen's risky choices, by designing a well-thought-out plan to protect her. You will also be able to silence the perfectionist voice in your head, and create a clear vision for both you and your daughter. And because parenting a teen takes much of your energy, we'll discuss why it's important to replenish your "I feel good" energy in order to be on top of your game and have something to give to your daughter. All of this empowers you to parent proactively instead of reactively. The added benefit for you is that you'll reclaim your life in the process.

In Part II, we give you help in rebuilding your connection with your daughter—the connection you had before she reached her teen years. When you are exhausted it's easy to get caught up in your daughter's drama, and over time that drama turns into predictable reactive patterns which I call the Drama Dance. This is why, when you regain your perspective and energy, it's easier not to lose control. The fact is, your daughter is hard-wired for drama, meaning that there are physiological reasons for her extreme mood swings and reactions. Because of this, she will make mistakes, which is why she still needs your guidance. Your daughter's mistakes don't define her; but they are useful in revealing where she lacks maturity. Understanding this allows you to guide, discipline, nurture, and protect her effectively. It also helps you to keep things on an even keel and see the opportunities for developing a more positive relationship with your daughter. You can intentionally create a new "dance," a new way of relating, between the two of you.

Finally, in Part III, you'll learn how you can start creating a new future for you and your daughter. This involves parenting proactively, intentionally, and strategically. Your focus is on all the possibilities for you and your daughter, rather than on the head butting. Your attention is on how your daughter can thrive and reach her dreams, which can lead to giving more consideration to your dreams as well. Part III is about how you can build a connection with your daughter that can last a lifetime. It shows you that this moment can be your turn too. Imagine leaving the resentment behind and living a fulfilling and enjoyable life during your daughter's teenage years. This is possible when *you* get back into the schedule, and you don't let everyone else's agenda drive your life. What's more, when you have created a life you love, you'll be more attractive to your daughter. She will want to hang out with you more, because she sees that you are more relaxed and are fun to be around.

Why I Wrote This Book

This book will set you free from worrying about whether you are a good or bad mom. In fact, "Am I a good mom?" is the wrong question. The question you should be asking is, "Am I an invested mom?" You can be your daughter's chauffeur and be busy dropping her off at activities, but not really be invested in her life. I've seen this over and over again. You can get so sick of the drama, and feel so hurt and betrayed, that you stop investing in the relationship. On the outside, no one would know. You're still cooking dinner and driving her to soccer. But inside, you may have checked out. You may have given up on getting your sweet child back. You may be counting the days until she leaves home. Maybe you're telling yourself this is okay because you'll reconnect when she is an adult. Perhaps you have resolved that this is how it is, but if you're honest, there's a sadness you carry around in your heart that you're not closer to your daughter.

I've written this book because I don't want you to give up on reconnecting with your daughter. I had a college girl in my office recently who told me she wished she could have a real two-way conversation with her mom. She wanted her mom to really listen to her instead of cutting her off or launching into a long monologue. Your daughter wants you to know who she is *today*. She doesn't want you to think of her only as the drama queen she was or the last mistake she made. What you think or believe about your daughter really makes a difference to her.

Being invested in your daughter is getting to know who she truly is and who she is becoming. It means suspending your judgments and listening to her heart. You invest in the relationship by intentionally creating good experiences. You maintain a respectful connection with your daughter even when she's not respectful.

I'm not saying this is easy. There are many challenges to maintaining a good connection, which is yet another reason why I wrote *Dial Down the Drama*. This book will help guide you through the complexities of the teenage years, and give you everything you need to have a richly rewarding relationship with your daughter and to enjoy those precious years that you have together.

I am not a perfect mom with a perfect daughter. I don't believe they exist. But I do know that I'm an invested mom. When I look back at these years with my daughter, I'm not going to remember the drama. I'm going to remember those ordinary moments that we got to share together. I won't forget my daughter's courage, creativity, compassion, humor, and bright spark. I'm going to cherish the many adventures we shared together. I will forever be grateful that I didn't miss these priceless years.

How about you? Reading this book is an investment for a busy mom that can change your life and your relationship with your daughter. Are you ready to dial down the drama and enjoy her teenage years?

PART I

Regaining Perspective
on Your Life as a Mom

CHAPTER 1

Are You "All Mothered Out"?

The red leather sofa in my office has supported hundreds of moms who are "all mothered out."

Janice, the mother of a teenage girl, kept checking her cell phone during our session, hoping her daughter would text. "I'm so stressed," she tells me. "I can't focus on my work or get anything done at home. I'm worried about my daughter all the time. She has this boyfriend drama and isn't getting her schoolwork done. I check Find My iPhone constantly when she's out driving and she's never where she's supposed to be."

Sharon, the mother of three, looks like she has it all together, with her perfect makeup, hair, and stylish clothes. But she's actually stressed and exhausted. "I just don't feel like myself," she confides. "I have so much going on that I don't have twenty minutes to sit down. My husband works late hours and it's all on me. I'm driving one teen to dance class, trying to make dinner, and helping the other two with their homework. I try to have a nice house, but it feels impossible to keep up with it. Seriously, I get so frustrated with my daughters. Is it really asking too much for them to put the dishes in the dishwasher?"

Susan, a single parent and cancer survivor, was widowed when her daughter was in middle school and last year, when her daughter was a sophomore in high school, her cancer returned. "I'm working full-time while going to doctors' appointments and receiving weekly chemo treatments," she explains, "and when I come home after work, I go straight to the couch. My daughter's not any help. Her room is always trashed. She doesn't even care enough about me to clean out the kitty litter box. "

Three different scenarios but the result is the same. Frequently our daughters leave us feeling all mothered out. Sometimes it's the stress of a daughter who is in full-blown drama and pushing you to the limits. Other times it's the day-to-day irritations of your daughter not doing homework, leaving her towels on the bathroom floor, and keeping her room so messy that you're not sure what's living in there.

Why We're All Mothered Out

The constant arguing, having to stay on top of their daughters' homework, listening to all the drama with friends and classmates, and going to bed worrying if they will turn out all right are just some of the reasons we feel all mothered out. But there are other reasons as well that have nothing to do with our teenage daughters. We have children, partners, extended family, and friends. We are weighed down with aging parents, financial pressure, work and family responsibility, and community involvement. Then there are unwanted seasons in our lives—going through a divorce, the loss of a job, or a serious illness.

Moms are pretty amazing but they don't have super powers. The problem is that you can give so much and get so busy that you lose yourself in the process, and when that happens, you deplete all your mothering resources.

Here's the dilemma that most moms face: to be the best possible mother for your daughter, you need to access your whole beautiful, passionate, playful, spiritual, creative, wise, spunky, reflective, and authentic self. Yet, too often these vital aspects of your personality feel superfluous and get neglected. If this continues over time, you start to lose your spark and something dies inside of you.

Think about this: Why are there so many unhappy mothers? It feels like this is becoming a national epidemic. When you get a group of moms together, are they singing "What a Wonderful World"? Probably not. There's a good chance they are complaining about their husbands, children, and everything else.

But many of you are living the life you dreamed of as a kid. You have the house, partner, job, and kids. You hoped for a girl and got one—so why are you not enjoying your life now?

If you are not relishing your daughter or these mothering years, it's *not your fault*. Moms have been given the wrong messages. Disempowering parenting messages are rampant in our culture, and they affect all of us.

It's not as if we choose these messages or beliefs—we inherit them. They are so familiar to us they feel like sacred scriptures. But they're not. They are twisting the truth. They take us down dead-end roads. They rob us of enjoying our life. They keep us so busy and preoccupied with worry that we totally miss this precious time with our daughters. I call these "Powerless Parenting Messages." Here's the first one:

Powerless Parenting Message #1:
You Should Be 100 Percent Committed to Your Family and Should Put Yourself Last

This message is ingrained in mothers. We all know that a good mom is fully committed to her family, and this is a good and noble thing. Every gesture of love you give your family matters significantly, even when nobody notices. Every child and teenager who has a fully committed mother is greatly blessed, as what you do for your family is invaluable—truly!

I don't have any problems with the statement, "You should be 100 percent committed to your family," but I do have a problem with the part that states you "should put yourself last."

Putting yourself last on the to-do list feels very practical. With only twenty-four hours in a day, it makes sense to prioritize the needs of your family first, right? You're a mom, for heaven's sake. Isn't this what you're supposed to do? But what I want to tell you is that doing this doesn't work, not for you and not for anyone in your family.

It doesn't work because you never get through the list! Everyone else's agenda clamors for your attention, and your needs keep getting bumped to the bottom. Let's face it: You know things are bad when the dog gets her teeth cleaned before you do!

Yesterday, a mom told me she was sick of being a mother Robot-ron. I call this a "Mother Machine." A Mother Machine neglects her physical, emotional, and spiritual health plus all those wonderful facets that make her *unique.* "I push through my day ignoring my feelings and I never sit down," this mom told me. But you're not the Energizer Bunny who can keep on going and going and going—you get my drift. If you do, in fact, keep going and going and going, then you'll likely be an Energizer Bunny who eventually blows a gasket and explodes, usually when trying to communicate with your daughter.

Let's say you take your daughter shopping and spend a small fortune on clothes. You willingly sacrifice your time and money to make her happy. In return, you expect your daughter to be grateful. Sound familiar? Later, when you ask her to help do something at home, she sulks and announces, "You're a terrible mother!" This is when the Mother Machine starts to break down. Her response breaks your heart or ticks you off (or both!), and when Miss Nasty mouths off, you're much more likely to lose your temper if you are emotionally spent and physically exhausted.

The crazy part about this Powerless Parenting Message is that, no matter how hard you try to meet your family's needs, you will always feel you are letting them down. You will never feel the satisfaction of a job well done, as you would after completing a work project, because your family's needs are never-ending and there will always be more asked of you.

This is usually the point where mothers turn on themselves. You beat yourself up because you can't get everything done and end up feeling like you've let your family down. You're hard on yourself because you don't feel happy, and then you "should" all over yourself. You think, "I should be grateful: I'm healthy. I have a job. I have kids and a house. I'm married (or, Thank God, I am not married)." But your soul doesn't buy it. Just like Sharon, you end up saying, "I just don't feel like myself."

At the core of this belief that you should put yourself last on the list is another Powerless Parenting Message. It is the main reason you get bumped to the bottom. Really, it's the reason everyone else makes it on the list but you. *(Warning: this message is harmful to your health.)*

Powerless Parenting Message #2: It's Selfish to Pay Attention to Me

Moms are petrified of being selfish. And when you're petrified, it feels like an all-or-nothing deal. Here's an example: "If I'm a good mom, I *can't* pay attention to me, because if I take care of me, then I'm not taking care of my family." This may feel logical, but it's not.

I encounter this all-or-nothing thinking frequently with the moms I counsel. When I suggest that they spend one hour a week doing something just for them, their immediate response is "I can't. It would be selfish. I have to take care of my family. There's no time. Everything will fall apart."

Now I know there are selfish moms, but this character trait is not found in most mothers. More often than not, a mother will starve herself of care like an anorexic starves herself of food. It reminds me of Jenny, a sweet sixteen-year-old girl I saw in my private practice. Jenny weighed 85 pounds and suffered from anorexia. She was afraid to put even a half teaspoon of butter on the quarter of a baked potato she *might* be persuaded to eat because she was convinced she would end up fat.

Of course, most people can see how irrational her fear was, but moms have an even higher-level fear of being selfish. Believe me, an hour a week of care and nurturing solely for yourself is not going to make you selfish. It may actually give you the energy you need to take care for your daughter and the rest of your family as a fully functioning person, instead of as a Mother Machine.

Believing the message "It's selfish to pay attention to me" will lead you straight to the Mom Phenomenon.

The Mom Phenomenon

I remember many years ago dressing my daughter in one of those cute pink girly dresses. (You know, the kind of dress that your friends gave you at your baby shower.) It was a typical day and I was taking my adorable fifteen-month-old baby girl to the grocery store. She looked fabulous in her matching pink dress and bow. She even had on those tiny frilly white socks and miniature shoes.

As I walked with her through the aisles of the grocery store my daughter received quite a bit of attention. People would smile and say things like, "She's so cute!" Then they would look at me and quickly turn away. This happened from the produce section, through the entire store, and all the way to the checkout counter.

I loaded the groceries and started the car. When I looked in the rearview mirror before backing out of the parking spot, I gasped. It was early afternoon and this was the first time I had seen myself in a mirror. Mascara that I hadn't washed off from the night before was smeared all the way down my cheeks. I looked like some heavy metal rocker after a three-hour concert!

All my attention had been focused on ensuring that my baby looked adorable while I disregarded my own appearance. Consequently, she looked fabulous and I would have scared Buffy the Vampire Slayer!

This is the "Mom Phenomenon." You think you're caring for yourself by focusing all your attention, energy, and thoughts on looking after the ones you love. But you're not! You have forgotten about the most important part of the equation . . . *you!*

Let's see how the Mom Phenomenon impacted Jane. Jane has one teenage daughter and one teenage son. She is married and works part-time. Jane is very considerate and would help anybody. She is a conscientious mom who makes sure her kids are well provided for.

The first time I met Jane, it looked as if she just had rolled out of bed. Her hair wasn't combed, she had no makeup on, and she looked wiped out. In our session, she admitted that she had been very unhappy, and though she lacked energy, she would doggedly plow through her days in her haste to get everything done. As a result, she didn't feel close to her husband or her kids.

Here's where I started my sessions with Jane. I asked her to think of her attention as a pie. How did she divide it? Who got the most attention and who got the least? How big a slice of attention did she give to the different facets of her life, including her kids, husband, work, church, volunteer activities, hobbies, leisure, and anything else that was a part of her life? Then I asked her to rank them by priority and roughly draw out the percentages on her pie graph.

This is a replication of Jane's "Attention" pie graph, which she completed in her first session. When you look at it, there should be no surprise she was depressed.

Jane's "Attention" Pie Chart

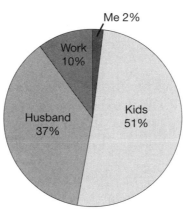

How about you? Do you know where your attention goes?

When you are caught in the Mom Phenomenon, you're not aware of where your attention goes because you're not aware of *you*. Jane was surprised at how little time she had for herself. No wonder she was feeling depressed and bitter.

How to Get Past the Mom Phenomenon

When you don't pay attention to yourself, you neglect your core needs. This creates a boatload of problems for you that will eventually spill over into your relationships with your daughter and others. See if you can relate to any of the statements that follow:

1. **No attention to *you* erodes your foundational health.** How often do you do any of the following in an average week?

   - You stay up late trying to get your work done, which leaves you totally exhausted the next day.

   - You try to relax but you end up drinking way too much, trying to unwind.

   - You know what foods are healthy but you end up eating a half-gallon of ice cream to make yourself feel better.

   - Even your "big" jeans don't fit any more and you can't remember the last time you worked out.

   - Every day is a "bad hair day" but you can't seem to make it to the hairdresser.

2. **No attention to *you* impacts your spiritual and emotional health.** As a result of taking care of everyone and everything else first, you . . .

   - Feel blah or exhausted all the time.

   - Feel trapped and you dream of escaping.

   - Are dragging through your days, just barely getting by.

   - Feel like you're going through the motions. Nothing feels meaningful.

   - Feel like you've let God and everyone else down.

   - Realize that no matter how much you accomplish you still feel like a failure.

3. **No attention to *you* damages your relational needs.** Forgetting to put your needs at the top of the list gives you permission to "fade" out of your own life.

    •   You don't return your friends' phone calls.

    •   When you do talk to your friends, all you do is complain.

    •   There is constant tension in your home.

    •   You're frustrated with everyone in your family and, while you're not the kind of person who gets angry often, you find yourself yelling at your daughter and later regret you lost your temper.

    •   Yes, you love your family, but you don't *like* them very much right now—and your favorite fantasy involves lying on a deserted beach by yourself with a pitcher of margaritas.

Here's the irony behind this "selfless" behavior: You sacrifice for your husband and kids in the hope that they will appreciate all you do, but you end up feeling let down, betrayed, and unappreciated when they don't give you the acknowledgment you feel you deserve. This is what happened to Mary.

Mary and her husband Bill have four children, ranging in age from seven to thirteen. Bill is very successful at his career and has provided a nice home for them. The only problem is that he works long hours, and it's not unusual for him to come home from work between eight and ten in the evening. Meanwhile, Mary is busy attending to her kids from morning to night. She is frustrated because she doesn't even have twenty minutes in her day when she can sit down and read a page or two in a book. All these little disappointments have added up to major resentment towards her husband. Every night, when he walks through the front door, she explodes and tells him how horrible her day was. She wants her husband to rescue her from this draining life, but instead he begins avoiding her by coming home even later from work.

Soon Mary's resentment was the size of Texas. Her husband walked in the house late one evening and she lit into him. "You don't help at all around the house. You don't appreciate all I do. All you care about is yourself. You are the most selfish person in the universe!"

She couldn't believe these words flew out of her mouth. The next morning he said, "I'm tired of being your emotional punching bag. I didn't get any sleep last night. I don't know if our marriage is going to work. I think we need to separate."

Mary was devastated, and she was already overwhelmed. She kept thinking, "I should be able to get everything done. I just need to be more organized." She felt like a failure as a mother and wife.

Mary had good intentions. She believed the Powerless Parenting Messages which told her to be "100 percent committed to your family and put yourself last" and "It's selfish to pay attention to me," so she ended up bitter and resentful, causing her husband to run for the hills.

Here's where I started my work with Mary. She needed a new Powerful Parenting Message to replace "It's selfish to pay attention to me."

Her new message became: "It's crucial to pay attention to me."

Mary started evaluating her situation. Her husband worked late hours and she knew that wasn't going to change. She realized there was really too much to do taking care of four kids and a large house. She realized she wasn't a failure; she just needed help. Once Mary got clear about her situation, she quickly decided she needed a full-time nanny and housekeeper. She approached her husband about this and he told her he was happy to write the check. She was shocked to learn that doing this was totally worth it to him. He truly wanted her to be happy.

Mary quickly found out that when she paid attention to her needs, everyone won. She had more patience with the kids. She enjoyed her husband and wanted to be intimate with him; he liked that. Before she knew it, the resentment dissipated and she started enjoying her husband and family again.

Perhaps it's time we moms developed a new message!

**Powerful Parenting Message #1:
It's Crucial to Pay Attention to Me**

Here's the bottom line: If you want to be a healthy, happy mom, it's crucial to pay attention to yourself. You can't wait for others to give you permission. You could be waiting a very long time. You have to own it and *give yourself permission,* because you know your physical, emotional, and spiritual health are crucial to you and your family.

There's no other way to do this successfully.

"I give myself attention. I get a manicure once a week," one of my clients told me on her first visit. At the same time, this mom was extremely stressed out. She yelled and overreacted with her kids. She didn't like being around her husband and was frustrated with her friends. She really knew something was wrong when she kept getting angry with her aging mother.

Clearly the manicure wasn't cutting it (pardon the pun).

Paying attention to yourself starts with being *aware* of your needs. This is challenging, because as mothers we have learned to ignore them.

Now at some level, you know your needs are important. A lack of knowledge isn't the problem; it's the lack of *awareness.* And when you finally look up from your distracted life, you can't believe how long it's been since you had fun, saw your best friend, or had a dental appointment.

This happened to me today. As I was writing this section of the book, the dentist's office called and told me it's been a year since my last visit. I'm wondering, How can that be?

Let's face it: Mothers are multifaceted creatures and we need to pay attention to each aspect of our lives. This is why we need a whole lot more than a new purse or a new pair of shoes to make us feel better.

The Five Essential Needs for Feeling Good

In order to feel your best, you've got to focus on five essential needs: foundational, maintenance, relational, personal enrichment, and spiritual.

Foundational Needs Satisfying your foundational, or physical, needs means getting back to the basics: getting enough sleep, taking time to rest, eating a healthy diet, and paying attention to the overall care of your physical body.

It has become "normal" for most moms to dismiss their foundational needs. We'll nag our daughters to get to bed at a normal hour while we burn the midnight oil trying to get everything done. This may be normal—but it's not healthy.

It's time to pay attention to your physical health. I know you know this. The problem is *you are not aware* of all the ways you ignore your body. Here are some questions that will help you become more aware of yourself.

Awareness Questions

- Do you get between seven and eight hours of sleep a night? Do you feel rested when you wake up?

- Do you have some downtime every week?

- Are you eating healthy meals and taking vitamins?

- Are you drinking enough water?

- Do you exercise? How often?

- Are you current with your medical appointments?

- How's your energy level?

Start by listening to your body. For goodness sake, if you need to go to the bathroom, *go!* If you are tired, go to bed. If you need rest, take a night off. If your body is aching, get a massage or go to the chiropractor.

Maintenance Needs Maintenance items are repetitive chores that need daily or weekly updating. Frequently, these items are on your to-do list. Mothers usually get a gold star in this category, especially when the items have to do with the family. But though we are aware of and attend to our family needs, we slack off when it comes to our personal maintenance. When it comes to family, here are some awareness questions you can ask.

Awareness Questions

- Do you have enough groceries at home to feed your family for the week?

- Do you keep up with the laundry?

- Are your house, yard, and cars in good working order?

- Are you current with paying the bills?

These items tend to be in the forefront of your mind because they also impact your families. They're important because they keep your family running smoothly. But maintenance items alone will not renew your heart, soul, and mind. That's where personal maintenance comes in.

Personal maintenance is whatever you define it as. For example, you may see manicures as part of your weekly maintenance, but for others this activity is not important. Or perhaps you see having a long, leisurely soak in a bubble bath as beneficial. The half-inch grey stripe in the roots of my hair lets me know I've been slacking with my personal maintenance. But whatever it is that causes you to feel relaxed and rejuvenated is what I'm referring to in this section. Try some of these awareness questions to see how you're doing in the personal maintenance area.

Awareness Questions

- Do you have regular hair appointments—or is every day a bad-hair day?

- Do you like your clothes? Do they fit you properly?

- Do you get your car washed and vacuumed regularly? How many empty paper cups and plastic bottles are in the back seat of the car?

Many of the foundational items, like eating healthy food, exercising, and downtime, can also be on your maintenance list.

Relational Needs Relationships are everything. They are what you hunger for. You want emotional intimacy with your husband. You desire to feel loved, encouraged, cherished, seen, understood, and appreciated. It's important to feel like you belong. You long for healthy relationships.

"I am with my family all the time. I am always relational," you may say. Well . . . yes and no.

You can spend much of your time "herding" your family (including your husband). Your conversations become "herding" conversations: "It's time to go to school." "You need to start your homework." "It's time to get to bed." "You need to clean your room."

These interactions are draining, to say the least. Though they are necessary, they do not build positive feelings. There are other ways to connect that are rewarding for you and your family, but for this to happen you need to be relaxed.

Awareness Questions

- Do you have downtime with your daughter daily?

- Do you have activities planned with your daughter that both you and she would enjoy?

- Do you have consistant dates with your husband away from the kids?

Let's look at friends and community, too. It's not good for you to be isolated, and yet too often that may be exactly what you do. You get caught up in the maintenance issues and blow off spending time with your friends.

Awareness Questions

- When was the last time you saw your close friends?

- Do you have a group of friends that you used to spend time with regularly?

- Do you return your friends' emails and phone calls?

- Are you intentional about making time for your friends?

Personal Enrichment Needs Personal enrichment brings beauty to your home, expands your mind, opens your heart, taps into your creativity, challenges you physically, and gives birth to your dreams. Sometimes it's just plain fun.

Personal enrichment feels good. You feel challenged, open, engaged, passionate, joyful, and content. Well, that may be asking a lot, but at the very least, it sure feels better than obsessing and complaining.

Personal enrichment is not a chore or an item on your to-do list. The desire comes from inside of you. It's what gets you out of bed in the morning and gives you energy to get through your day. You could be planting flowers or listening to a lecture, but you lose track of time. You are in the creative flow. Personal enrichment activities make you feel like yourself. They recharge you even more than a manicure or massage.

Given how helpful this area is, it's ironic that personal enrichment is the number one area mothers give up or neglect. It feels like it's not important and therefore optional. You feel like it's selfish. But personal enrichment is *crucial* for your happiness. There are physiological reasons for this. Personal enrichment gives you experiences that increase the happy body chemicals known as seratonin and dopamine. (Stress and drama decrease these chemicals.) And we need to "stockpile" these happy chemicals to better weather the adolescent storms.

Personal enrichment is . . . well, personal. It's what *you* like. It speaks to *your* heart. What's enriching to someone else may not be enriching to you.

Awareness Questions

- Do you enjoy how your home is decorated?

- Do you spend time developing your creative gifts?

- Do you plan activities that are fun for you?

- When was the last time you read an inspirational book?

- What used to challenge you or bring you satisfaction before you became a mom?

- If you didn't have to be "perfect" at doing something. what would you like to try?

Spiritual Needs It's important to pay attention to your spiritual needs. You can go to your particular house of worship seven days a week and still feel disconnected from yourself and God. To feel connected to God (Higher Power, Universe, Spirit, the Divine . . . however you choose to label the transcendent), *you need to be connected to yourself.* This is the only way to have a personal relationship with God.

Time for personal reflection is essential. If the speed of your life is 100 miles per hour, you will have a lot of activity but you will miss the important things of your life.

There's the "fish in water" syndrome. A fish is not concious of water because it's always *in* it. You can be so *in* your life that you don't have perspective. When you are swimming in a river of sadness and resentment and are feeling overwhelmed, you go through your days feeling bad, and if you are not careful, this can become your new normal.

Personal reflection keeps you from settling for less than you deserve. It allows you to step back and name your feelings, thoughts, and experiences. It gives you perspective. You see where you are and where you need to go. It allows you to be honest with yourself and forgive yourself and others.

Only when you are aware can you change your situation. This is where healing starts. This is where the Divine can break through. This is the soil for personal renewal.

Awareness Questions

- Do you have time to be quiet and listen to your heart?

- Do you have a consistent spiritual practice? This might be prayer, meditation, reading, or a gratitude journal.

- When was the last time you had a big "aha!" moment about your life?

- Is your heart in an open or closed place?

- Do you recognize God moments (you might call them "synchronicities")?

Where Do You Start?

"Holy moly! I'm totally overwhelmed. I'm already way too busy. There's no way I can pay attention to all these areas. That's impossible."

Don't worry. This is just the beginning. This new Powerful Parenting Message, "It's crucial to pay attention to me," is your compass. It will lead you in the right direction. The first step (and it's a big one) is your awareness. I don't want you to feel overwhelmed. This book will break things down into practical steps and lead you into developing a new "normal," all the while providing you with practical suggestions and the clarity you need.

Now, let's start small.

Pick one thing in each of the essential needs areas that you can implement this week. This is totally doable. It really won't take a lot of time, it takes just a little bit of your attention.

Here are some examples:

- **Foundational:** Drink four glasses of water a day.

- **Maintenance:** Buy new underwear. Throw out the ones with stretched elastic.

- **Relational:** Email your friend about getting together.

- **Personal Enrichment:** Make a trip to the nursery and buy azaleas for your flower bed.

- **Spiritual:** Spend five minutes at night writing three things that you are grateful for in a journal.

In order for you to implement this exercise you need another Powerful Parenting Message.

Powerful Parenting Message #2:
Commitment to Yourself Is the Foundation
for Commitment to Your Family

Let me restate this another way: Commitment to yourself doesn't replace your commitment to your family; it's *the foundation for* your commitment to your family.

There is power in *your* commitment. This is because you are making a promise to yourself. You will be loyal to your family and to *yourself.*

To be committed to yourself means . . .

- Take it slow and start small.

- Do it imperfectly.

- Forgive yourself.

- Take it step by step.

- Be kind to yourself.

- Celebrate small victories.

- Invest in yourself.

- Show up.

- Receive help.

- Take action.

Commitment to yourself enables you to feel like your healthy, playful, wise, powerful, creative, and authentic self by *taking action.* It allows you to bring all these vital aspects into your parenting, and when that happens, everyone wins.

How to Get Your Partner on Board

"I don't think my husband will go for this." He will and here's why. Your husband doesn't benefit when you follow the Powerless Parenting Messages. You are no fun to be around. You're not the woman he married. He's sick of you complaining and attacking him for every little thing. He feels your resentment and frustration. He knows you don't want to be physically intimate with him.

Connect the dots: If Mama ain't happy, ain't nobody happy!

He *wants* you to be happy. He'd do anything to have you stop criticizing him. Instead, offer him a practical solution. Present your solution without the drama. Tell him, "I need to start paying attention to me. This doesn't mean I'm going to do anything crazy. I'm still committed to our family, but I need to start exercising. I need to see my friends. I may need some extra help a couple of hours a week."

Give him concrete examples so his imagination doesn't go wild. Connect the dots by saying, "I know I can be cranky. This is because I'm exhausted. I'm going to start taking care of me and what you'll get is a happy, contented, amorous wife." He'll quickly see the advantages.

* * *

It's time to replace the old Powerless Parenting Messages with new Powerful Parenting Messages. The old messages drain you emotionally, physically, and spiritually, leaving you all mothered out. No one benefits when you don't feel like yourself and are reduced to a Mother Machine.

A great mom is not a machine; she is a healthy, multifaceted human being. It's time to get *you* back with the new Powerful Parenting Message #1, "It's crucial to pay attention to me." Paying attention to yourself is not selfish, quite the contrary; it underpins a commitment to yourself. And when you embrace Powerful Parenting Message #2, "Committment to yourself is the foundation for committment to your family," everything starts to shift for you and your family.

If mama's happy, then everyone's happy!

CHAPTER 2

What Fear Does to You and Your Daughter . . . and What You Can Do About It

I enjoyed seeing Nancy again. Two years earlier, I had coached her through a messy and unwanted divorce when her daughter Brittany was in middle school. During that time, I was consistently impressed with Nancy's authenticity, courage, and stellar sense of humor. I witnessed her let go of life as she knew it and courageously begin again as a single parent.

Five months ago, Brittany was caught sexting with her eighth-grade boyfriend. Nancy immediately brought her to see me. Brittany is not a bad kid. Like many girls, her boyfriend bullied her and demanded sexual pictures, and she gave in. She worked hard in therapy and, after four sessions, she decided to break up with her boyfriend.

Yesterday, Nancy sat on my office couch and at first appeared to be her jovial self. Then her face tensed up. "I'm at a breaking point," she admitted. I asked Nancy what was going on. "I just can't let it go," she told me. "I'm stuck in protective mode. I can't relax. Brittany has another boyfriend. You think I'd get a break. The summer was awful, I had to make sure Brittany was busy all the time, and now she just started high school. I keep thinking she's doing something that she shouldn't—that she's being sneaky. I'm so afraid that Brittany is going to get hurt, her life is going to be ruined, and it's going to be my fault."

Nancy didn't know it then, but she'd been hit with the "F-bomb" (the fear bomb.) The F-bomb is fear to the tenth power. The fear is so big that it dominates your thoughts and takes over your life. It becomes panic.

"I didn't know it was fear at the core," Nancy said. "It was masked. Fear is so insidious and sneaky. I thought I was just in protective mode, but I couldn't stop. I kept thinking that I'm not being vigilant enough. I would constantly drill my daughter about what she was doing. I couldn't get enough information to satiate my fear. And then she would back away from me, and I felt like *crazy mom*, but then her backing away made me think, she really is guilty."

Fear not only impacted Nancy's relationship with her daughter, but it was affecting the rest of her life. "This is embarrassing," she told me, "I've been to the emergency room twice in the past couple of months. One night I fell down the stairs. Another day I had fifty-nine things on my mind and I ran into the door. I'm exhausted. I can't sleep. I drink too much wine and eat way too much comfort food, but that doesn't make the fear go away. Because I don't have a partner, the weight is so heavy on my shoulders. I can't live this way anymore."

I felt a lot of compassion for Nancy. I've experienced the F-bomb with my own daughter. One night, after my daughter's first breakup, she stayed out way past her curfew. I texted and called her but she had her phone turned off. This was at a time she was especially fragile and I had no way to get hold of her. I panicked. It felt like something horrible had happened to her. My worst fear was that she could be dead. In the middle of the night I drove around Houston aimlessly for an hour with tears streaming down my face. I kept looking for her car and never found it. When I finally got home, her car was in the driveway and she was asleep in her bed.

Nancy is not crazy. The F-bomb impacts us all. Fear is amplified in our culture with stories in the media of date rapes, suicide, eating disorders, drunk driving, school shootings, drug addictions, and teenage dropouts. This is why it's easy for our imaginations to go to the worst possible scenario.

It doesn't matter if it's an actual threat or an insubstantial fear, it's going to impact you the same. The F-bomb invades your thoughts and takes a toll on your body. But the good news for Nancy and every other mom is you don't have to be held hostage by fear. "You don't have to live this way," I told Nancy. "This fear can be tamed, but first you have to understand how it impacts your brain."

How Fear Impacts the Brain

Let me give you some brain basics to help you understand the F-bomb. Fear triggers the limbic system of the brain. Think of the limbic system as a car. The amygdala, the integrative center of the brain for emotions, emotional behavior, and motivation, is the driver of the car and is constantly scanning for danger because it wants to keep you safe. If the amygdala perceives a threat, it presses down the gas pedal of the hypothalamus, which releases stress chemicals such as adrenaline and cortisol. Now the car is stuck in overdrive. Scientists call this the *stress response*. It's a helpful response if someone tries to steal your purse. You need all those chemicals to fight the attacker or to run away as fast as you can. But we moms of teens can live in perpetual stress response with all the tragic news in the media about teens keeping the threat of potential danger in the forefront of our minds.

The problem is that when you are in stress response or emotionally flooded with other negative feelings like anger, sadness, shame, or panic, the limbic system takes control and automatically presses the *off* button to the cortex, which is your higher brain. The cortex is composed of the prefrontal cortex and the right and left hemisphere. The prefrontal cortex is called the executive region. It is the master control center of the brain and coordinates and balances what happens in the brain, nervous system, and body. The right hemisphere enables you to see the big picture, generate solutions, tap into your intuition, and be creative. The left hemisphere is dominant for language, and logic, as well as literal and linear thinking. When the limbic system is in control, so much of the good stuff from the prefrontal cortex and the right and left hemispheres goes offline that you are literally not dealing with a full deck.

The limbic system is the reactive part of the brain, and when you get triggered you are not consciously aware of it. Like a fish in water, you are swimming *in* fear. Nancy was right; fear is sneaky and insidious. Most of the time you are not conscious that you are *in* stress response. You think you are protecting your daughter. But this limbic, fearful state significantly impacts how you interact with your daughter. You can't access the perspective, intuition, creative problem solving, and logical and rational thinking of the cortex. What's left is the limited responses of fight, flight, or freeze. These responses are physiological reactions that occur in response to a perceived harmful event, attack, or threat to survival. These responses become a huge problem when the perceived threat is to your daughter, or her safety.

The Limbic Dance

Your limbic response quickly activates your daughter's limbic response, and in short order these interactions become predictable patterns. These patterned responses repeat and escalate in hopes of bringing about a resolution, but to no avail. For example, if your response is to fight, your daughter responds by fighting back, taking flight, or freezing up, or some combination of the three. Her reaction escalates your stress response and, therefore, you fight back. These back-and-forth exchanges turn into what I call "the limbic dance."

Fight When you are in fight response, you are ready for battle. Your body is jacked up with adrenaline and other body chemicals. Because of this, it's easy to lose self-control. You raise your voice, slam a door, or throw something across the room. Words fly out of your mouth that criticize, belittle, shame, and threaten . . . and it's hard to stop.

Kim told me how her seventeen-year-old daughter, Camille, had come home at 5:00 A.M. Mom and dad had been up most of the night calling her friends trying to locate her. When her daughter casually walked in the house, mom lost it: "Where the hell have you been? You are so selfish and mean. Do you know what you put me through? I hope you have a kid as heartless and cold as you."

No teenager is going to say "Thank you, Mom. I understand why you're angry. You just want to make sure I'm okay. You're right, it was selfish of me." They are going to strike back in fight response. As a mom, I can understand Kim losing it, but talk about bad timing! Camille was tired and drunk, so rather than responding rationally, she yelled, "You wonder why I didn't come home. You're f***ing crazy. All my friends hate you." For the next week, both mom and daughter kept their distance from each other.

Fight mode doesn't have to involve a frontal attack ("Where the hell have you been?"), as this next story shows.

While on the surface Nancy didn't lose self-control, on the inside she was a mess. Because her core fear was that her daughter was not okay, she kept firing questions at her daughter. Of course there's nothing wrong with asking questions. The problem is that their whole relationship was reduced to mom grilling Brittany about her plans. Brittany's reaction to mom's constant interrogation was to stay in her room, lock the door, or give mom one-word answers. Every time Brittany avoided her mom, Kim's fear increased, and so did the monitoring of her daughter. You can see how this limbic dance spirals out of control.

Flight We all need a break from all our responsibilities. Moms especially need breaks from theirs, and even more, they need breaks from their daughters. Vacations, time with friends, downtime, and solitude are necessary to rest and recharge. This is healthy, and it is not a *flight* response. A flight response is when you distance yourself from your daughter because you are emotionally done with the drama. This feeling can be conscious or unconscious. It feels too hard. You are tired of the constant worry and stress. You give up. You say things to yourself like, "She's made her bed, now she has to lie in it. She'll be gone soon. There's nothing I can do anyway."

Bottom line is that the fear feels bad, and you want to avoid the source of pain. You try to forget about your problems by becoming distracted with other things in life. It's like you resign from your mother job a little too soon. I have seen many a mom distance herself from a difficult daughter by having a little fling with someone she works with.

The problem is that when you take flight, you leave your daughter unprotected because you're not paying attention to her.

You have a vital place in your daughter's life, especially now. Though she acts more autonomous and leans on her friends, she still needs your love, understanding, attention, input, guidance, and protection.

Your daughter is never going to say, "I need you to be there for me. You're ignoring me, and that hurts my feelings."

But she could do something big to get your attention. She could . . .

- Come home two hours after curfew.

- Sneak out at night—*and* take the car.

- Become a drama queen.

- Fail a class—or several.

It will escalate until she gets your attention. As hard as you try to escape your situation, the fear for her is still there. That's why you are taking flight.

Freeze The freeze response is when you are literally paralyzed by fear. It's like your whole body shuts down. You can't focus because your thoughts are racing. You don't know what to say or do, except worry. Moms frequently default to the freeze response when they are dealing with a strong, fiery daughter who uses threats and intimidation—in other words, who is always in a fighting mode.. These girls learn that they can get their way when they fight because their moms freeze up.

Let's face it, many of our teens have an inner mean girl. Unfortunately, this has become the norm in our culture. Teen girls can fight dirty, using psychological warfare. They do this through emotional blackmail.

Emotional blackmail is manipulation through threats and intimidation. Your daughter wants her way and she amps up the fear and anxiety to a point you can't say no to her. You're caught in a double bind. If you enforce guidelines or boundaries, you feel like something terrible is going to happen. This leaves you feeling helpless, heartbroken, and confused.

She may threaten to . . .

- Leave home.

- Drop out of school.

- Do drugs.

- Live with the other parent.

- Not talk to you again.

- Hurt or cut herself.

She may intimidate you by . . .

- Yelling and losing control.

- Slamming doors.

- Throwing things.

- Physical intimidation (like pushing or cornering you in the room).

- Verbal abuse.

Shelly is a recent widow and mother of Amy, her thirteen-year-old daughter. Shelly is doing as best she can, working full-time and raising her daughter by herself.

Her daughter was not in a good place. Amy used hard drugs, cut and burned herself, skipped school, and made one suicide attempt. Amy also frequently visited an online sexual chat room.

I asked Shelly if she knew about Amy's behavior. She quickly let me know that she wasn't a "helicopter mom," a mom who constantly hovers over her daughter, and that she wasn't "heavy-handed." I asked if she had any concerns about Amy. She casually told me that she didn't like Amy going to the sexual chat room. She described an episode where they were sitting on the sofa, and she glanced over at Amy's computer screen. She saw a message that said, "Show me your boobs." Then she watched her daughter type back, "Go f*** yourself." Shelly did nothing about this.

Shelly's reaction didn't make sense to me. Why would an educated mother who deeply cared about her daughter not protect her? It looked like Shelly didn't care. Nothing could have been further from the truth. In actuality, she was completely overwhelmed and paralyzed by fear. Her limbic reaction was a freeze response.

Shelly was intimidated by and afraid of her daughter. Amy had a hot temper and would rage and throw things. Shelly was scared her daughter would actually hit her.

Shelly was also afraid *for* her daughter. She was afraid to set limits because Amy threatened to run away. This brought up sheer panic in mom. She had already lost her husband. How could she lose Amy too?

The sad truth is that mom's freeze response left her daughter unprotected. Her daughter's life was in real danger, with the drugs, cutting, sexual promiscuity, and suicide attempt.

It's not Shelly's fault. No mother intentionally freezes. It is a horrible place for a mom to be in. You feel like you can't do anything, yet you feel the weight of danger. The good news for Shelly is that she received the help and support she needed. Now, four years later, Shelly has her power back and Amy is sober and thriving in school.

Underneath all the fight, flight, and freeze responses is a Powerless Parenting Message.

Powerless Parenting Message #3: It's My Job to Worry and Obsess About My Daughter All the Time

It feels like it's your responsibility to worry and obsess about your daughter all the time. One of my clients said it this way: "I feel like if I worry enough I can protect my daughter; if I don't worry, something bad will happen." This is a very common feeling for moms. It *feels* true, but it's *not* true. Constant worrying and obsessing is a sign that fear is driving your life and your parenting. Fear hijacks you and sets you on a downward limbic spiral. You think you are protecting your daughter, but actually the fear hinders your ability to keep her safe.

To turn this around, you need to know what fear is driving you.

How to Move Past the Fear

You can't completely eliminate the fear, but you make it more manageable by dismantling the F-bomb. Next, you need a new Powerful Parenting Message that steers you in the right direction. Finally, you can use the two tools I'll give you to redirect your attention away from the fear to what is real and positive. Let's look at these one at a time.

Dismantle the F-Bomb

The F-bomb is overwhelming. When the fear is so big, and you have countless worries, it's easy to get paralyzed. To dismantle the F-bomb, you must identify the *big* fear. Then the constant worry and obsessions need to be contained so they don't take over your life. Finally, you want to excavate the truth from the fear in order to discover the real concern.

Identify the **Big Fear**   Take fifteen minutes, find a quiet place in your house, and ask yourself this question: What is the *big* fear concerning my daughter? Is it about her health, safety, or her future? Most often our biggest fear can be boiled down to "My daughter is *not* okay, and will *not* be okay."

Let's go back to Nancy. After the sexting incident with her thirteen-year-old daughter, Nancy's big fear was that Brittany would get pregnant. That fear impacted how Nancy interpreted Brittany's behavior. If she rolled her skirt up a little high, mom thought, "She's trying to get knocked up." If her daughter didn't answer her text, she thought her daughter was having sex with her boyfriend and "was getting knocked up." This fear was driving Nancy's life and she didn't even know it. This biggest fear multiplied into thousands of worries a day.

Contain the Worry and Obsessions The big fear takes over your thoughts and actions through worry and obsession. The problem is that worrying over your daughter 24/7 is not good for your health, and it won't protect your daughter. Worry and obsession throw you into a stress response, which increases the stress hormone cortisol, which in turn decreases all the happy body chemicals, which further lowers your mood. Increased cortisol also compromises your immune system and is responsible for weight gain. The bottom line is that constant worrying makes you feel bad and is exhausting.

Worrying and obsessing will not protect your daughter, because when you're in stress response you're offline from your higher brain. With the limbic system in control, your thoughts are repetitive and negative and the same worries play over and over in your mind. It feels like you're taking action because the obsessing takes up so much of your mental space, but you're not.

Another problem with worry is that it has an active imagination. You create multiple distressful or horrible scenarios in your mind. Then your mind settles on one devastating story and replays it over and over. Now your worry has an obsessive quality to it because you fixate on one thought or story. Not only do you think about it, you feel it. When you picture your daughter in this horrible situation you suffer, feel panic, and experience distress. How could you feel such intense feelings if it were just your imagination? Without the grounding of your higher brain, all these imagined scenarios feel true. In other words, your big fear is now a full-blown blockbuster movie that you watch repeatedly in your head, and which always ends badly.

Not only do you think and feel these worries, you act on them. But your actions will always be ineffective when you're offline from your higher brain. We've already discussed the stress responses of fight, flight, or freeze. Your action has a compulsive element as well. You do something over and over again but it doesn't bring relief, results, or resolve any of the issues. A common example of this is checking. Moms find that they can't stop checking their daughter's phone, stories, grades, or room. Yes, it's important to monitor your daughter, but this is where you can get stuck being her twenty-four-hour monitor. Don't become Monitor Mom—it really doesn't work. This compulsion to monitor her never allows you to rest. Cindy was worried about her teenage daughter, and during our entire session, her head was down looking for a text from her daughter. Though I gave her good counsel, she couldn't take it in due to her constant checking. Even though we may feel that being hypervigilant is a good thing, our compulsive action often blocks us from receiving the information we need.

When Nancy was worried about Brittany, she described an unquenchable need to *know more*. This had become a compulsion. She searched the Internet for research on sexting and teenage pregnancy. Instead of calming her, the information gave her more things to worry about. This became a cycle, as increased worry caused her to search for more information.

While you can't get rid of worries completely, you can learn to contain them. Instead of being preoccupied with worry all day long, try taking fifteen minutes and giving the biggest fear and its attendant worries your complete attention. Because worry is hiding in the background of your mind, you need to stop doing everything else to bring it into full awareness. It's like a computer virus that's completely eating up your memory. You don't know something's wrong until everything starts to shut down. In the same way, you may not be aware of how much worrying is affecting you until it impacts your daily life.

Bring the worry into your consciousness in those fifteen minutes. Go to a place where you won't be distracted, and write down all of your worries. Don't rush this. You want to make sure you give all your concerns your full attention. Now you're ready for the next step, which is excavating the truth.

You may think, "I don't have time for this," but actually this exercise saves you time. By giving your complete attention to your worries, you're done for the day. Though the worries will come back, you can say, "I've already dealt with you, there's nothing more to worry about today."

Excavate the Truth from the Fear Now that you've given your worry your full attention, you want to extract the truth from the fear. The way you do this is by asking yourself three questions:

1.   Is your fear really true?

2.   How likely is it that this is going to happen?

3.   What's the real concern?

You need to get the higher brain online and all its functions in order to dismantle the F-bomb. These questions activate the logical side of the left cortex. Let's see how they work in the following examples.

Example: Your daughter, who has been scraping by, failed a major chemistry test.

> *Your big fear:* She won't get into a good college, and will end up being a loser.

> *Your worry:* You picture her going to the community college and hanging out with the wrong people. You imagine her taking off with a guy on a motorcycle with sleeves of tattoos. You picture her getting pregnant. You worry about what your mom will say when you take her home at Christmas, big belly and all.

Example: Your daughter, who is 5 feet 3 inches and weighs 135 pounds, ate the entire big bag of Cheetos in one sitting—plus a half a bag of Oreos.

> *Your big fear:* She is going to end up obese and alone.

> *Your worry:* The kids at school will make fun of her and call her names. She won't be able to play volleyball. No one will take her to the prom. Even if she is invited, will she find a prom dress that fits? She better make good grades so she can support herself, because no one wants to marry a fat girl. I'm so sad that I will never have grandchildren.

Now let's see those three questions in action.

1. **Is this really true?** When I ask clients if their fear is true when they are in full-blown panic, they'll say, "Yes, it's true." Then I will ask them if they absolutely know that their daughter will end up a poorly educated loser, or obese and alone, and they will say no they can't know that for sure, but then they quickly add that it *could* happen. This is where you need the next question.

2. **How likely is it that this will happen?** It's not likely that if your daughter fails one test she will end up an out-of-wedlock pregnant failure. Nor is it likely that your high-end-of-normal-weight daughter (remember "pleasingly plump"?) will end up obese and unloved—much less that there isn't a beautiful prom dress out there for her. Ninety percent of the scenarios we make up in our mind never happen.

3. **What's the real concern?** The real concern is that your daughter is on the way to failing chemistry, and she needs help with this class. The real concern is that your daughter will become a compulsive eater and will battle with weight her entire life. If she gains much weight, her health will suffer, The real concern is always specific and can be measured. When you're able to accurately identify the problem, what to do becomes clear.

You can download a Dismantle the F-bomb Worksheet from my website, at www.colleenogrady.com/bookresources.

Now that you've dismantled the F-bomb, it's time to replace the Powerless Parenting Message with a Powerful one.

Powerful Parenting Message #3:
I Trust My Inner Wisdom to Take Effective
Action to Protect My Daughter

Bear with me as we analyze this message phrase by phrase.

I trust my inner wisdom . . .

Webster's dictionary describes wisdom as a "knowledge that is gained by having many experiences in life; the natural ability to understand things that most other people cannot understand"; "good sense or judgment"; and the "ability to discern inner qualities and relationships." This wisdom is available to you when you are back online with your cortex. Only then will you feel centered and able to access it.

Use your inner wisdom to:

- See the whole picture, without excluding information.

- Remember the beauty, wisdom, talents, strengths, potential, and the positive things in your teenage daughter, even though there are inevitable mistakes, challenges, and shortcomings.

- See everything in context, without blowing things out of proportion.

- Remember that your teen is not fully developed; she is a work in progress.

- Be open and reflective—and admit when you are wrong.

- Seek out help and support, and know you can't do it alone.

- Know when to speak and when to hold your tongue (no matter how hard); when to wait and when to act.

- Tap into your intuition, faith, and spirituality.

. . . to take effective action . . .

Determining the real concern enables you to take effective action. The more accurate and specific you are about the problem, the more on target you'll be about what to do.

If you're concerned that parents won't be at the party your daughter wants to go to, the next step is clear. You find out if the parents will be home. Your inner wisdom tells you how to get that information. Once the F-bomb is dismantled, you'll know what to do. You call the parents, or go to the door and meet the parents when you drop your daughter off.

Effective action isn't waiting for the other shoe to drop, it's being proactive. You not only anticipate upcoming problems but you have a strategy in place to deal with the problems. Effective action is not just focused on the challenges. It targets ways to help your teen thrive. This strategy looks at every aspect of your teen's life from health, academics, social, talents, and abilities. This gives you a blueprint for action. This is such an important concept that I've dedicated an entire chapter to how to create your personal proactive parenting strategy (see Chapter 10).

. . . to Protect My Daughter

Protecting your daughter can feel completely overwhelming. It can feel like all the responsibility is on your shoulders. Moms often feel this way because they know all the ins and outs of their daughter's life. Plenty of times I've heard moms complain that their husbands were clueless in regards to their daughters. They felt the dads stepped in and made things worse. Oftentimes, dads just need you to fill them in on the pertinent information.

It really does take a village to raise a teenage daughter. Having support calms the fear. You can rest because you know that all the players are in place. This can include friends, family, coaches, teachers, tutors, religious leaders, and professional help. Later in this book you'll learn how to build your Daughter Team (also in Chapter 10).

And now, as promised, tools to help you move past the fear.

Two Tools to Tame the Fear

When you're stuck in worry mode, it's like your mind is trapped in a dark cave. These tools will help bring back the light and hope. They'll help you see the beauty in your daughter again by switching your focus from what you don't want (worry) to what you do want (love and optimism), from imagined fears to the present, real strengths in your daughter.

Create a Prayer or Affirmation Write down all your worries and fears on a piece of paper in pencil. Leave a space between each line. Make sure you take some time with this exercise. You want every single one of your worries written down.

Now go back and write what you want underneath each fear. If you're afraid your daughter is going to fail her classes, then write: *My daughter works hard at her classes and makes good grades.* Or you can write it as a prayer: *God give my daughter the strength and discipline to work hard on her classes and reach her potential.*

Too often, our prayers are focused on the negative and just keep our attention on the fear: *God help my daughter not get raped and killed* keeps your imagination on her being raped and killed. This does not bring you any comfort.

After you turn around every worry and fear to what you want, erase them so that all that you're left with is your positive affirmation or prayer. I've been doing this for years. I start each day reading my affirmation as a prayer. It reminds me of what I really want and helps me stay centered.

Focus on Growth, Gratitude, and Gladness We miss so much that is positive when we obsess on our fears. This exercise redirects your attention. Instead of looking for negative evidence, you start looking for positive attributes. Go out and buy a journal and label it "Growth, Gratitude, and Gladness." Every night write one thing down in each category. It doesn't matter how small; everything counts.

- **Growth:** Where do you see growth in your daughter? Did you see your daughter make an effort today? *My daughter did the dishes without my asking.*

- **Gratitude:** What is one thing in your daughter that you are grateful for? *I am grateful for my daughter's sense of humor and that she makes me laugh.*

- **Gladness:** What about your daughter brings you joy or delight? *I love how she takes hilarious pictures of my dogs and texts them to me.*

* * *

The F-bomb brings devastation to your family. You can't completely remove fear from your life, but you can move through it. Fear is useful when you're able to identify the real concern, and can then put an effective plan in place to protect your daughter. But who wants to live in continuous stress response? By containing the worry, you'll find that you'll never have to be held hostage by fear again.

CHAPTER 3

Why Moms and Daughters Can't Get It Right All the Time

Most people would think Sharon is the ideal sixteen-year-old. She's a straight A student in her accelerated classes. She takes dance classes and is an improving pianist. She has a good group of friends and doesn't drink or do drugs. Yet, Sharon is stressed all the time. It's rare that she relaxes because she constantly feels pressured to improve her grades, dancing, and proficiency on the piano.

Janet, her mom, describes her daughter this way: "Sharon is argumentative, stubborn, and needs to control her anxiety. It's so frustrating; when I give Sharon suggestions she just blows up and is incredibly disrespectful."

Sharon admits her mom drives her nuts. "I just can't get anything right. Mom thinks there's a right way to do everything. She doesn't bend. It has to be her way. My mom was the perfect child and thinks she is the perfect mom. As hard as I try to please her, I feel unworthy." When I asked Sharon if she really thought her mom was perfect, she said, "She tries to be, but she has a hard job, comes home in a bad mood, and takes it out on us."

Many of us can relate to Sharon's mom. We try to get everything right, but at the end of the day we go to bed frustrated. We wake up and it's still there—the pressure to be perfect.

Where the Pressure to Be Perfect Comes From

We live in a culture that holds moms to a perfectionist standard that is unattainable. No matter how hard we try to reach the bar, we are destined to fall short. The media, movies, TV, beauty industry, and advertising all tell us that we need to look and act a certain way in order to be happy and successful. What's implied is that if you don't achieve perfection, you are a failure.

No mom—self unfortunately included—wants to feel like a failure, so we just try harder. You push yourself hoping to get to a place where the pressure lifts, but no amount of activity gets rid of it. No matter what you do, you feel you are falling short. You ask yourself, "Why can't I get it together?" or "What am I doing wrong?"

Instead of evaluating what's wrong with you, evaluate what's wrong with the cultural message. The message is flawed. The perfectionistic standard will never bring you success and happiness. Let's explore how this next Powerless Parenting Message fuels the pressure to be perfect.

Powerless Parenting Message #4:
Mothers Are Supposed to Do It All and Get Everything Right

Cathy is married and the mother of two daughters, one a freshmen in high school and the other in middle school. Because her husband has been out of work for the past three years, she is working full-time, in addition to handling most of the responsibilities around the house and with the kids. "I'm doing a terrible job as a parent," she said. "I'm so disorganized. I struggle to stay on top of the girls' homework. They go to different schools and it's hard to get them to school on time. After work, I'm rushing to get one to soccer practice and the other to ballet class. I can't seem to spend the quality time I want with my daughters. I tried getting up earlier, to make the lunches, but it's still hectic." Cathy wasn't doing a terrible job; she was a loving compassionate mother. Nor was she disorganized. She believed she was, though, because she was trying to do it all with little support from her husband. Cathy was beating herself up because she believed the wrong message.

Although you know it's impossible to do it all, you keep trying. You joke (and complain) about having to be Supermom, but you still think it's possible. You think that if there were more hours in the day, you would be able to do it all. You think that you should be more organized, that you should stay up later to get more accomplished. You feel pulled between work, home, and a myriad of other commitments but, despite all your sacrifices, you end up feeling that you haven't done enough.

While getting everything right feels like a gentler and more realistic goal than being perfect, it's really the same thing. It means being perfect in all areas of your life. It's easy to see the absurdity of this message when you step back and evaluate it.

Let's start with the idea that a perfect mom has perfect hair and a perfect body. This means, for example, that you're never allowed a bad hair day. (Let's just say I've already failed the test.) Yesterday I picked up an advertisement for lingerie in my mailbox. On the cover it said, The Perfect Body. Behind those words were several young female bodies with legs that were the size of their arms. Obviously they had been Photoshopped. How can you compete with that? Why would you want to? The models can't even compete with their own Photoshop images. Against such images we all fall short.

You're supposed to have the perfect spouse and live in a perfect house. Both you and your husband are expected to work at the perfect job with perfect hours and salary. You need to be efficient and productive while balancing the demands of work and home perfectly. At night you're expected to transform yourself from mom to hottie with ample libido to satisfy your partner at any and all times. And it goes without saying that if you're a perfect mom, you have perfect kids.

Let's think about how crazy this message is. There aren't enough hours in the day to be perfect in all areas of your life. If your house is clean, your hair and weight are perfect, and your daughter is being an absolute angel, but you forget to do something at work, you still fail because you didn't get *every*thing perfect.

Let me ask you a question. How do you feel about the "perfect" mother at your daughter's school? She's nice to everybody and is in great shape. She has a successful business and has an amazing husband who is her soul mate. She lives in a great part of town with a tastefully decorated house. Her kids are happy, well liked, good at sports, and successful in school. Are you happy for her? Probably not!

Have you ever thought why it's so easy to criticize "perfect" people? It's because their very existence makes you feel bad about yourself and your family. You constantly compare your waistline or the size of your home. When someone has a smaller waist or a bigger home, you feel diminished.

Your daughter feels the same way about the popular, beautiful girl who makes great grades and is dating the good-looking, smart, athletic guy. She compares herself to this girl and blurts out, "I hate her. She's perfect!"

This perfectionistic standard sets up a fierce competition that drives you to constantly measure yourself against other people. If your friend is more productive, beautiful, and talented, you feel bad about yourself. If your daughter is making A's, and your neighbor's daughter is failing a class, you feel better about yourself. This constant comparison is a breeding ground for criticism, resentment, judgment, and blame.

The truth is that even those we perceive to be at the top of the food chain have this gnawing feeling that they are not measuring up. No one can "do it all and get everything right." Basing your self-worth on this message will take you straight to Mother Shame.

The Impact of Mother Shame

In *Daring Greatly,* Brené Brown, a research professor at the University of Houston Graduate College of Social Work, defines shame as "the intensely painful feeling or experience of believing we are flawed and therefore unworthy of love and belonging." I define Mother Shame as "the persistent gut-wrenching feeling that you're flawed as a mother and failing everyone in your family." Mother Shame says that you are the problem. This horrible feeling keeps you from being authentic with other moms. You're afraid to be real because you feel you're the only one who can't get it together. This is a normal feeling among moms of teens. I can't tell you how many times in my practice I hear moms say, "I'm so relieved. I thought I was the only one."

Believe me, you're *not* the only one. This is a cultural problem. When we see the big picture, and speak our truth with like-minded moms, we're set free from this shame. The challenge is that when you're in Mother Shame, it feels personal. You feel you are the only imperfect one and that you don't belong. Then you internalize the shame through the Sneaky Mean Voice, the continuous running commentary in your head.

The Sneaky Mean Voice

Here's why I call this voice "sneaky." Most of the time, you're not conscious the voice is there, but it's babbling away in the background of your life. You may be doing the laundry or on a conference call at work while the voice is pounding away at you.

The voice is mean. Psychologists call it the "critical inner voice." But it's more than critical; it's your worst enemy. The messages are cruel, debilitating, and knock the wind out of you. The mean voice looks for opportunities to attack.

- Mean Voice *criticizes* you: "You're an idiot. You can't get anything right. You're a loser."

- Mean Voice *mocks* you: "Of course she doesn't listen to you. You don't have a clue."

- Mean Voice *questions* you: "Why did you do that? Why did you open your mouth?"

The Mean Voice disempowers and maintains the Mother Shame. Like fear, shame causes us to go offline from the higher brain. You're stuck reacting, obsessing, and compulsively reaching for the unattainable bar of perfection in hopes of silencing the Sneaky Mean Voice. But as long as you believe Powerless Parenting Message #4, you won't be able to silence this voice.

The Sneaky Mean Voice shakes your confidence, so you look for validation from outside yourself, be it from husbands, family, mentors, or other moms. This can cause a whole new set of problems. When you put so much value on what other people think or expect from you, you can lose yourself in the process.

But the biggest trap for moms is when you look to your daughter for validation.

Do you grade yourself as a mom by how well your daughter is doing? This feels logical. You think, "If my daughter is making good grades and is respectful at home, then I'm doing a good job. If she fails a test or has a drama fit, then I get an F on my mom report card." Here's the problem, though. You see your daughter in a number of situations throughout the day. Each interaction becomes an invitation to judge yourself to see if you're "getting everything right."

- "If my daughter is always polite and respectful, I'm getting things right."

- "If my daughter is happy, I'm getting things right."

- "If my daughter obeys me and behaves, I'm getting things right."

- "If my daughter makes good grades and excels in sports, dance, music, or theater, I'm getting things right."

- "If my daughter is popular and has lots of friends, I'm getting things right."

- "If my daughter has the perfect weight and is in shape, I'm getting things right."

You can't let your self-worth be dependent on your daughter's performance or mood. If you do, her success or failure becomes about you, and the only way you can escape Mother Shame and feel good is if your daughter is perfect.

This is a huge setup for the limbic dance. Your daughter's imperfections trigger Mother Shame because you feel like a failure. Now the problem has become much bigger than your daughter failing a test or coming home late. This feels like an attack on you, and your limbic system is primed to fight, flight, or freeze.

Powerless Parenting Message #4 doesn't work for you, nor does it work for your daughter. One of the most detrimental parts of this message is the pressure it puts on her. Just like you, she can never live up to this message.

The Myth of the Perfect Daughter

There's no such thing as a perfect daughter. She does not exist. A teenage girl is hard-wired to be imperfect because her physiology is undeveloped. That's why she still lives at home and needs your guidance and protection.

Janice has a seventeen-year-old daughter, Wendy, who just finished her junior year in high school. During her sophomore year, Wendy made good grades, worked hard at dance, and was every mom's dream kid. She was polite to her parents and they could trust her. Last year, Wendy left her small conservative private school and went to a large public high school. It was hard for Wendy to make friends at first, but then she started hanging out with the party kids. She met her boyfriend there, who had a reputation for being quite the player. Janice was concerned about Wendy's new group of friends and started to monitor her more closely. Wendy lied to her parents in order to hang out with her friends, and it didn't take long before Wendy was caught in a big lie with her boyfriend.

Janice's devastation quickly turned to anger. "After the incident I can't believe anything she says," she told me. "What bothers me the most is that my daughter isn't who I thought she was. I used to see only the good qualities in Wendy, and now I see her as a *liar.*" Janice said she told her daughter that she could never look at her in the same way because she was a liar. Wendy crumbled under her mother's disappointment and became seriously depressed. She started hiding in her room and cutting herself.

It's hard when our daughters disappoint us, but they will. This is normal, and in later chapters I will talk about all the good things that come from mistakes. Your daughter needs to struggle and makes mistakes in order to find her autonomy. But the perfectionistic standard is so deep in us that we find ourselves constantly let down by them. How we handle disappointment is of utmost importance because, left unchecked, it creates bigger problems, which is what happened with Janice and Wendy.

Janice experienced Mother Shame, and then shamed her daughter by labeling her a liar. The shame blinded Janice from all of Wendy's positive qualities. She could only see the big mistake. As a result, Wendy experienced shame because of mom's blatant disappointment. Mom thought that being *tough* on her daughter would get her to change, but the opposite was true. According to Brené Brown, "Shame corrodes the part of us that believes we can do better, When we shame and label our children, we take away their opportunity to grow and try on new behaviors. If a child *tells a lie,* she can change that behavior. If she *is a liar*—where's the potential for change in that?" Nothing positive comes from shame. "Shame is positively correlated with addiction, depression, aggression, violence, eating disorders, and suicide."

This situation with Janice and Wendy turned around when Janice understood the real enemy—the pressure to be perfect. She saw that her reactions originated from feeling flawed as a mother. When Janice opened up to Wendy about her own vulnerabilities, Wendy softened and let her mom back into her life. Eliminating the shame shifted everything. Janice began to understand her daughter in new ways. She realized Wendy was extremely hard on herself, and though it looked like Wendy didn't care, in truth, she was struggling with this pressure. These realizations fostered a more authentic connection. They started enjoying their time together, Wendy's depression lifted, her grades improved, she stopped the cutting behavior, and she was accepted to a prestigious university.

The Pressured Daughter

The perfectionist standard hits hard on the teen culture. Girls feel the pressure to look the right way and have the right jeans, shoes, dress, underwear, hair products, phone, computer, and nail polish. They feel the pressure to have the right grades, friends, and boyfriend, and to get into the right college.

Something that may not seem like a big deal to you can be huge for your daughter. A bad hair day won't ruin your life, but may seem catastrophic to her. She can spend hours in front of the mirror to make sure that every hair is just right. The issue really isn't hair, but the pressure to look a certain way so she won't be ridiculed in school.

The pressure to be perfect is hard on you, but it's even more intense for your daughter. You have life experience and a fully developed brain. Your teenage daughter, having just gone through puberty, is dealing with many issues for the first time, such as having a fully developed body, and romantic interest. Issues like self-esteem and belonging take on a whole new meaning in the teenage years. School can feel like a battleground for her worthiness. If someone has better grades, is more outgoing, and wears a size smaller jeans, your daughter's self-esteem plummets. How she feels about herself becomes all about comparison, which creates a fierce and mean competition among her friends. It doesn't matter where girls are on the popularity scale, there's always somebody more beautiful, talented, and successful to compare themselves to. With this constant pressure to be perfect, your daughter can never rest or feel good about who she is or what she has accomplished.

Your daughter has a Sneaky Mean Voice as well. Her running commentary sounds like, "You're fat, ugly, stupid, weird, and are a loser." Frequently, girls will project their inner mean voice onto others in order to boost their self-esteem. They will ridicule and put down other kids, or attack you in order to feel better about themselves.

Parents are often unaware of how much additional pressure they put on their daughters. Rachel is a sophomore in high school. "My parents are so hard on me, "she told me. "I would bring home a ninety-one on a test and my mom would say I could do better. They would get angry at me if I didn't make an A. Nothing I did was good enough. They would say, 'You're a good kid but you need to make better grades, enjoy church, join more clubs, have more friends, and be in the top one percent of your class.'" I asked Rachel how the pressure impacted her. "I'd get really stressed out before I'd take a test because I felt pressured to make a good grade," she said. "I would second-guess myself and get really confused. Then I'd feel really horrible and sad that I made a bad test score and I would hide my grades from them. I'm scared to talk to my parents." Her parents did find out about her grades and got extremely angry. They told her she was a bad kid.

Too much pressure translates into increased anxiety, which lands you in one of the stress responses. Rachel hid her test grades, taking *flight* from the problem, would *freeze* when she was taking the test, and when she would get tired of her parents getting down on her, she would *fight* back. When Mother Shame meets Daughter Shame, there's going to be drama.

My daughter once said to me, "You think you're so perfect." Believe me, I know I'm not perfect. What this meant was that she felt judged by me or that she was judging herself. But for whatever reason, she felt shamed. This was the last thing on earth I wanted her to feel. I didn't react. I used this as an opportunity to talk about the big picture. We talked about the pressure to be perfect and how this unreachable standard affects us all. I was able to show up in a real, authentic, and vulnerable way. This allowed my daughter to see me as a person, not just as her mom. The irony is that my vulnerability motivated my daughter more than any lecture I could have given her.

How to Create a New Culture for Moms

It is time to create a new culture for moms that replaces unreachable perfectionistic standards with those that are attainable. This is not about resignation in any way; it's about a resolve to be your very best self. In this new culture success is redefined. It includes imperfection because none of us walks through life perfectly. It's not uncommon for our imperfections to give us the life lessons we need to be successful. Our babies didn't learn to walk by taking perfect steps. None of us would have learned to walk if that was the case. Babies learn to walk because we cheer them on every step of the way, even when they fall. Create a new Mom Culture with this message.

Powerful Parenting Message #4:
Healthy Mothers Accept Their Imperfections, Strive to Do Their Best, and Model Moving Forward

Accepting your imperfections doesn't mean you are condoning your mistakes. It means that you are liberated from the harsh judgment of Mother Shame. Imperfections are not the end of the world; they are part of the journey. With eyes of compassion, you will be able to identify the blessings that come from your imperfections.

Accept Your Imperfections

My most popular Facebook status to date is, "The goal is not to be a perfect mom and have a perfect daughter, the goal is to love our daughters and believe in them, in their imperfections." I think so many moms Liked this because they are tired of the pressure to be perfect. It's really not the goal. Loving your daughter and having a healthy connection with her is the goal. When you start being kind and loving to yourself and give up the goal of being the perfect mom, you can accept your imperfections. This will change your inner dialogue. You can replace the Sneaky Mean Voice with a Kind and Loving Voice. You can give yourself grace and compassion. Whatever voice you listen to is the one you will project onto others. If you're kind to yourself, you will be kind to others; if you're harsh with yourself, you'll be harsh with others.

It's a relief when you can lay down the yoke of perfectionism and accept your daughter as she is. When the pressure is off your shoulders to have a perfect daughter, you can begin to enjoy her again. You can see that her worth has nothing to do with perfectionism. Her self-esteem comes from knowing she's loved. Love is what motivates. All that good stuff— forgiveness, authenticity, grace, compassion, caring, and understanding—comes from love. Knowing that her mom is on her side and believes in her empowers your daughter to get back up again when she falls. When someone knows all our messy parts and still loves and believes in us, it makes us unstoppable.

Your daughter needs to know she is loved unconditionally, even with her imperfections. She needs to know she is loved even if she fails, makes mistakes, or disappoints you. Unconditional love is the foundation for your daughter being creative, trying new things, and challenging herself.

Imperfections are not the end of the world. It's what we do with them that matters. If we accept them, they can bring us all sorts of gifts. Failure is an opportunity for creativity and innovation. There are many blessings that come from imperfections: authenticity, forgiveness, freedom, love, creativity, courage, perseverance, and resilience.

Our worth, health, success, and happiness have nothing to do with being perfect, though our culture would make us believe they do. All of us are on a journey. Many of our imperfections and failures become the stepping stones to our success. Human beings are resilient. We are able to become strong, healthy, and successful again and redeem our mistakes. It was my struggles and imperfections as a teen that enabled me to be a youth minister, coach, and therapist.

Yes, we are imperfect, but there's an amazing treasure in all of us. Sometimes it's hard to see the treasure in our daughters, but it's still there. It's just buried under the drama, attitudes, failures, and mistakes. But unconditional love is the only way to excavate the gold.

Strive to Do Your Best

Julie is married with one daughter in high school and another in college. For the past four years, she struggled with intense Mother Shame because of her college daughter's earlier behavior in high school. Julie tried to numb the shame through food. But this created a whole new set of problems, and in the next four years she gained a hundred pounds. The weight was affecting her health. She had knee problems and would get easily winded. I asked Julie what she wanted. She told me she wanted to improve her health and go on a vacation with her husband. I suggested she get on the treadmill for one minute a day, and she agreed. The next week, she told me (with a big smile on her face), "I did it!" Building on her success, I continued to challenge her one minute at a time. By the end of the next four weeks, she had increased her time to twenty minutes a day. And, yes, she was able to go on vacation with her husband.

Julie was a completely different person in six months. She started smiling again. Her confidence came back, and she reconciled with her daughter. What made the difference? She silenced the shame through this message. Healthy mothers strive to do their best.

- **Striving to do your best is about *your* best.** The starting point is *you,* rather than comparing yourself to others. You are not trying to reach the unattainable cultural standard. You define what your best is, and are only in competition with yourself. For Julie, this was getting on the treadmill for one minute a day.

- **Striving to do your best is doable.** No matter how hard you strive to reach perfection, you'll fall short—always. In contrast, striving to do your best is completely doable. Increasing her time on the treadmill one minute at a time was doable for Julie. She changed her life by focusing on what she could do. Her attention was on what she was doing right, instead of where she fell short.

- **Striving to do your best is hopeful.** Julie saw she was making progress. This built up her confidence, which motivated her to take another step. She could see that she was moving forward because *she* was the starting point. If she missed a day, it didn't matter because she could see how far she'd come. Perfectionism feels impossible because you compete with the superstars. There's a huge chasm between where you are and where you're supposed to be, with no clear steps to get there.

- **Striving to do your best feels good.** Julie came back with a huge smile because she was proud of what she had accomplished. She gave herself credit for each small step, even if it was only the extra one minute on the treadmill. Striving to do your best allows you to celebrate the victories, no matter how small. In contrast, if you feel you can never get everything right, there's no celebration. If one thing isn't right, it invalidates the 95 percent that *is* right.

- **Striving to do your best is kind.** Instead of being barraged by your Mean Voice, you are kind to yourself. Your inner voice is gracious and encouraging. "At least I got some help." "I did it!" "I missed a couple of days but at least I was able to work out three times this week." This is important because when you are kind to yourself, you extend that kindness to your daughter. This allows you to see your daughter with new eyes. You see her small victories. You recognize that she is striving to do her best.

Model Moving Forward

About a year ago, I was missing my daughter (a very busy senior). At 9:30 one night she texted me and asked me to take a ride with her. With the windows down, sunroof open, and music blaring, we drove off in her red beetle through downtown Houston.

"I was thinking about who could I talk to about this," she said, "and even though you're my mom, you're the best person. Mom, I want to make a big difference in the world. I want to inspire as many people as I can not to give up on their creativity. We're kind of the same. You speak to lots of moms, and are writing your book. You want to change the world and so do I. I want to learn how to speak. Where would I start?"

I was shocked. This really blew my mind because it came at the end of a very difficult year with my daughter. Her year started with a heart-wrenching breakup. There were lots of hard moments as well as a few good ones. But my daughter knew I loved her, even if I didn't always get it right. I would like to think that my big elegant mother lectures changed her life, but that's not true. What helped my daughter move forward was watching me be authentic, be vulnerable, admit my mistakes, and not take myself too seriously. This enabled my daughter to open up because she could identify with me. I realized she was watching me closely, even when I thought she didn't hear a word I said. She saw me develop my creativity and take risks. She watched me feel scared, fail, and get back up again. She watched me celebrate my victories. This gave my daughter permission to take imperfect action.

You model moving forward not by being perfect, but by being authentic, owning your imperfections, and striving to be your best.

You model moving forward by:

- Sharing imperfect stories. "I got a D in Spanish my sophomore year in high school."

- Telling vulnerable stories. "John broke my heart when I was sixteen and he started dating my best friend."

- Being willing to laugh at yourself. "Look at these pictures from the 80s. What was I thinking? Look at how huge my hair is with that perm."

- Sharing your little successes with her. "I made it to the gym today."

- Celebrating your big successes. "I got a book deal!"

- Being a lifelong learner. "Look what I learned on the guitar."

You also model moving forward by how you treat your daughter when you're angry, frustrated, hurt, or disappointed in her. The question is not solely, "Is my daughter getting it right?" The question is, "Am I modeling who I want my daughter to be?"

* * *

We live in a culture that holds us to an unattainable perfectionistic standard. The result is the "pressure to be perfect." This impacts everything, especially our parenting. We feel the pressure and pass it down to our daughters.

Stop being a prisoner to this pressure. Accepting your imperfections, striving to do your best, and modeling moving forward can free you from perfectionism. This is not a one-time decision, but a daily practice. The benefits are well worth it.

Once the pressure lifts from your home, you'll be amazed at how it will change the atmosphere. Instead of heaviness, you and your daughter will experience joy, laughter, and love again.

CHAPTER 4

Why Your Clarity Matters

Rushing home from work to get dinner started, Cathy stops at the grocery store to pick up some milk and other items. As she walks down the produce aisle, she hears her cell phone ring, answers, and hears her daughter sobbing loudly, "Mom, where are you? I can never do anything! Why won't you let me go to the party?" "What party, Jill?" Cathy asks while picking up carrots, lettuce, and tomatoes for their salad. "You're so stupid!" Jill yells into the phone as mom pushes her grocery cart down the next aisle. "I don't know what you're talking about," Cathy replies. Her daughter hangs up on her.

Now mom is mad. To make matters worse, when she gets to the car Cathy can't find her keys. After taking everything out of her purse and still not finding them, she calls her husband and asks him to bring her spare set. Dave arrives ten minutes later, opens the car and, as they start loading the groceries in the back seat, sees her car keys at the bottom of the grocery basket. He tells her she needs to be more organized, and as she drives home Cathy stews over Dave's comment. Her thoughts briefly turn to all the things she does for her daughter, before she remembers that she forgot to finish a report at work that is due the next day. As if that's not enough, when Cathy pulls into the driveway, she sees that her gas gauge is on empty, which means she will have to leave early in the morning to fill up. As she empties the bags of groceries, she realizes she forgot the milk.

Cathy's confusion and forgetfulness is what I call Mother Fog. It occurs when there are so many things going on at one time that you can't think clearly; it happens all the time with mothers. It's like your mind is covered with a thick, soupy, dense fog, and your thoughts, feelings, decisions, and actions are unfocused.

Mother Fog not only leaves you feeling scattered but it impacts your confidence. I've listened to many moms berate themselves because they "just can't get it together." Mother Fog is a trap that many moms fall into which hurts both mom and her family.

You can't live a fulfilling life and parent effectively if your clarity escapes you. Your clarity is the roadmap that lets you know where you are and where you want to go. Your clarity is the essential ingredient that eliminates 90 percent of the drama with your teenage daughter.

When Your Clarity Can Escape You

Busy schedules have become the norm in our culture. We live our lives at 90 miles per hour. Speeding through our days, trying to get everything done, we end up multitasking, only to find ourselves in Mother Fog. We splatter our attention between home, yard, kids, work, spouse, friends, parents, religion, and volunteer activities. It's no wonder we can end up staring inside our refrigerator for several minutes in a complete trance.

There are many reasons for Mother Fog—exhaustion, fear, and pressure. But the root problem is that we've lost our center and disconnected from our self. We're no longer anchored in our mind, body, and spirit. We're tossed about on the waves of everyone's expectations for us. We've become a Mother Responder or a Mother Reactor.

Mother Responders

A Mother Responder is one who accurately identifies the wants and desires of her family and is able to appropriately respond to those needs. This is deeply engrained in most moms' DNA. This is a wonderful quality. Moms have a great capacity for empathy, and it enables them to anticipate the demands of those they love.

Starting as a young mom you learned to discern the specific cries of your baby girl. You knew whether she needed milk or to have her diaper changed. Now that your daughter is a teenager, you're still finely tuned into her nuances of tone, speech, and behavior and can anticipate her needs. You know how she is doing by the way she opens the door or by the music she's playing.

You not only anticipate the needs of your daughter, but those of all the important people in your life. You think about what's going on with everyone. It can sound something like this:

> Is my mom okay? Do I need to be with her at her next doctor appointment? My husband sure is edgy; what's going on with him? Has my daughter started her homework? She has a big math test tomorrow. I'm worried about my friend Mary. Is her marriage going to make it? When was the last time our dog had her flea treatment?

The ironic thing is that *you* are missing from your mental conversation. Your head is so filled with everyone else's needs that there is no room for you.

Your family likes your attention and benefits from it. Your kids, partner, or friends let you do the work and the worrying simply because you will and they don't want to. Your self-absorbed teenager is going to be all about her. She definitely will not be able to identify your needs. If you're tired and snap at her, she won't think, "Mom does so much; it's no wonder she's tired. I'll help her out." She'll just think, "Mom's in a really bad mood" or "Mom hates me."

This doesn't mean that you don't matter to others; they're just not thinking about your needs. A big reason is that you aren't clear about what you need from them. Our Powerless Parenting Message #2 from

Chapter 1, "It's selfish to pay attention to me," adds to this. If you aren't clear about your boundaries and what you need, your family and friends will expect more and more from you. If you continue to comply, you'll end up being resentful, frustrated, angry, bitter, depressed, and deeply hurt. And you will default to being a Mother Reactor.

Mother Reactors

You are a Mother Reactor when you're so stretched and stressed you can't fake it any more. You're just trying to get through the day and, because you have no reserves, it's easy to react and lose your patience with the people you love the most.

Juanita is married, works full-time as an accountant, and has thirteen-year-old twin daughters. Her husband travels during the week for work. For the past six months, Juanita has also been taking care of her mom, who is going through chemotherapy. Juanita brought her daughter, Maria, to see me because she was depressed.

I asked Maria what was going on and she said, "Mom's been in a real bad mood lately. She's been getting home late. She slams the door open and just starts yelling at us, 'Is your homework done? Why is your stuff all over the house? Why haven't you done your chores?' My mom never asks me how I'm doing. If I try to tell her what's going on with me, she says, 'Stop complaining; it's no wonder you don't have any friends.'"

Later I met with mom. I asked her what was going on. "I do so much for my family, and they don't do anything for me. My husband is as bad as the girls. He comes home on Thursday after being out of town all week and empties his suitcase onto the floor. It'll sit there all week until I clean up after him. My girls just sit around and watch TV after school, while the house is a mess. Then I have to cook dinner. I'm behind at work. I hate my life."

When you are a Mother Reactor, you find yourself reacting in all areas of your life, but especially with your teenage daughter. Here's what happens when Mother Fog meets teenage daughter.

Mother Fog and Teenage Daughter

When you are in Mother Fog you're at a disadvantage. Your daughter has the upper hand because she is crystal clear about what she wants. She is clear about . . .

- What she wants to do on the weekend.

- The kind of clothes she wants.

- What she and her boyfriend can do together.

- How late she wants to stay out.

- How she spends her time.

Her clarity will trump your fog every time. (Remember this; it's really important.)

What your daughter is *not* clear about is what is important to you. She feigns being foggy about when her assignments are due, whether she has homework, or what her chores are. And Mother Fog opens the door to drama. Here's why. Your daughter knows when you're in Mother Fog and will try to take advantage to do what she wants. She has an arsenal of tactics to get you to see things her way.

She will use forceful tactics and . . .

- Argue with you. "Why won't you let me go to the party?"

- Throw a drama fit. She will slam doors, sulk, shout, follow you around the house, and badger you to let her go. "Seriously, Mom, I *have* to go to this party."

- Shame and belittle you. "Mom, you're such a loser. Just because you don't have a social life doesn't mean that I shouldn't."

- Threaten you. "If you don't let me go to the party, then fine, I won't go to school. I don't care anymore."

- Punish you. She will let you know she is unhappy. "I hope you're happy. You've ruined my life."

- Withhold her attention. She'll avoid you, hide in her room, and if you ask her a question she will give you one-word answers. "Fine."

She will use "logical" tactics and . . .

- Use comparison. "Every other mom is letting my friends go to the party but me. Even Dad thinks it's fine."

- Prosecute you. "Give me one good reason why I can't go to the party."

- Be reasonable. "I know you don't want me at a party without adults supervising, but John and his friends will be there." (John is the host's twenty-year-old brother—that's supposed to reassure a mom?)

- Manipulate you. "No one likes me but Beth. If I don't go, then Beth won't be my friend and I won't have any friends at all. If you cared about me you'd let me go."

When all else fails, she will pull out the "nice" tactics and . . .

- Be complimentary. "Hi mom, have you lost weight? That dress looks great. Can I go to the party?"

- Be helpful. "Hey mom, I cleaned the kitchen and folded the laundry. Can I go to the party?"

- Bargain. "I'll clean the bathroom and do the dishes if you'll let me go to the party."

When you are in Mother Fog, your daughter's tactics can wear you down. Because you don't have any reserves, you are more likely to give in. You just want the drama to go away. But if you give in to your daughter's tactics, she will keep using them because they work.

The good news is that when you are clear-headed, your daughter's tactics won't work on you. Your clarity empowers you and eliminates a boatload of senseless drama.

The Road to Clarity

The road to clarity starts with knowing where you are and what you want. To do this, you turn the attention back to you in order to reconnect with your thoughts, desires, values, needs, feelings, hopes, wisdom, and intuition. Clarity is an ongoing process. Just because you were clear last week doesn't mean it carries over to this week or the next.

Know Where You Are

The first step to clear the Mother Fog is to know where you are. This takes time, reflection, honesty, and courage. If you don't take time to evaluate where you are, life has a way of stopping you in your tracks. This is what happened to Sarah.

Sarah's daughter, Rachel, was a cheerleader, well liked, and a junior in high school. Rachel had her own car and had a lot of independence. Sarah taught first grade, but her husband had been recently laid off. Sarah worried about her husband, their finances, and her job responsibilities. She was definitely in Mother Fog. There were signs that Rachel was struggling. Her grades dropped. She stayed out to two or three in the morning. Marijuana was found in her car. Mom had an uneasy feeling that something was wrong, but the fog pushed it away.

Rachel asked her mom if she could see me. During our session, Rachel revealed that she was in a dark hole and was scared. She was addicted to hard-core drugs and was partying in the apartments of thirty-year-old drug dealers. Because of her cravings, she kept putting herself in danger. When I brought mom into the session and Rachel told her what was going on, mom was devastated. I helped her get Rachel into drug rehab. It was a painful wake-up call but mom got crystal clear. Rachel changed schools and, after she was out of rehab, she joined an alternative peer group and remained sober.

The Mother Fog had hindered Sarah from knowing where Rachel was, but Mother Shame was also at play. Mom didn't want to admit that her daughter was having a drug problem. It can be difficult to admit that we need help when someone we know and love needs our help.

Knowing where you are starts with being gentle with yourself. You identify the problem areas but also remember the positive. You evaluate what's not working in your life but also remember what *is* working. Here's the paradox. If you ignore where you are, you'll be stuck there. The only way you can be where you want to be is to be honest about where you are. Asking questions like these can help:

- How is my relationship with my daughter?

- How is my daughter doing? What are my concerns?

- What's going well? What's not going well at home?"

- How do I feel about my parenting skills?

Know What You Want

The next step once you know where you are is to know what you want. Moms frequently tell me, "I don't know what I want." I believe what they really mean is, "I gave up on having what I want." Over time, moms slowly resign themselves to how they think their life is going to be. After years of constant drama, they stop believing change is possible. They are also used to tuning in to everybody else's needs but their own. Knowing what you want is like a muscle that has atrophied because it hasn't been used for a long time.

I'll make it easy on you. We'll start with what you don't want.

What Don't You Want? Let's start with your relationship with your daughter. Finish these sentences. (It should come easy to you.) You'll find two sample answers below each question.

1. I don't like it when my daughter _____.

   Throws her towels on the floor and leaves half-eaten pieces of pizza in her room.

   Doesn't come home on time.

2. I don't want my daughter to_____.

   Ignore me when I ask her to do something around the house.

   Yell at me and slam the doors.

To find what you want, turn this around. If you don't want your daughter to ignore you, what do you want? If you don't want her to throw her towels on the floor, what do you want her to do?

You also learn a lot about what you do want when you pay attention to what you complain about. You complain when your needs are not being met and you feel powerless to change things. On a sheet of paper, write down everything that bothers you about your daughter. Yes, I'm giving you permission to do some full-blown complaining. Now reread what you wrote. Make a list of your complaints. Then rewrite your list and turn your complaints into what you want. For example:

- *Complaint:* "My daughter doesn't do anything around the house."

- *What I want:* "I want my daughter to clean her room once a week. I want her to load the dishwasher after dinner on weeknights. I want her to walk the dog twice a week."

It's easy to get in the habit of complaining because it takes less thought and it's easy to vent. You think you're clear when you complain, but you're only clear about the problem and not about what you want to do about it. All your attention is on the problem, not the solution. Knowing what you want does take more mental energy, but the effort is well worth it.

What* Do *You Want? Part of knowing what you want is to know who you want to be. Who do you want to be as a mother, partner, family member, friend, or coworker? How do you want to come across to people? How do you want to appear to your daughter? For example, you might say, "I want her to perceive me as a calm, kind, fun, loving, and strong mother."

Now, let's look at what you enjoy. When I ask a mom this question, she often looks at me with a blank stare. After years of taking care of her family, the things that she enjoys have gotten bumped off the list, and she can scarcely summon up the memories of what she used to like.

On a sheet of paper, make a list of fifty things you enjoy. The reason I say fifty is that I want you to be specific. The more specific you can be, the better. For example, "I like to go on vacations" is too general. Instead say, "I enjoy a relaxed Saturday brunch drinking cinnamon coffee with my friend," and "I like the cool wind and the sounds of seagulls and waves crashing along the shore as I take my schnauzer for a late afternoon walk."

Here's one more question to help you identify what you want. On a sheet of paper, write down twenty things you would like to learn or do. For example:

- "I would like to learn how to play piano."

- "I would like to start riding my bike."

- "I would like to go on a retreat with a group of friends."

- "I would like to work out."

And finally, again on a clean sheet of paper, write two paragraphs. The first should focus on what you want for your relationship with your daughter. The second should focus on what you want for your daughter.

Knowing where you are and what you want is the foundation to knowing where you are going. You do this through intention. You can download my "Road to Clarity Worksheet" at www.colleenogrady. com/bookresources.

How to Turn Your Clarity into Intention

You can know what you want for yourself, but that's not enough to get you to where you want to go. You can want something, but your inner antagonist can find a million reasons why it won't happen. For example:

- "I want a good relationship with my daughter, but she won't talk to me."

- "I want to be happy again, but as long as my daughter keeps lying to me, it's not realistic."

- "I want a job that's more interesting (or pays better), but I didn't finish college."

It's not enough to just "want" something. You need to turn your clarity into intention. This involves combining clarity with resolve, deliberateness, determination—and action.

You don't get clear about your intention while driving through Starbucks. You find your intention by slowing down and being still. To live well, you need to be still every day, even if it's only for five minutes locked in the bathroom. Find what works for you. It could be morning walks with your dog, working in your garden, or prayer and meditation. In the stillness ask yourself, "What is really important to me? What do I want more than anything else in the world?" If your answer is, "I want to enjoy my teenage daughter," your next thought may be a rebuttal. "But that won't happen." Past experiences may remind you of the fights, the nights she didn't come home, and the mean things she said.

This is where faith and courage step in. It takes faith to believe there is more than the dissatisfying life you're used to. Courage and faith sounds like this: "Yes, things have been bad in the past, but that's not what I want. From this day on I will enjoy these years with my daughter." And now it becomes your intention: "I intend to enjoy these years with my daughter."

The Five Benefits of Intentions

I was talking to one of my clients about intentions and she said, "Well, that sounds like work." It's true; to live intentionally does take reflection, and forethought. At one level it is easier to stay stuck in your normal ruts and have your life run on automatic pilot. But that's not the life you want. To move forward in your relationship with your daughter—and your life—takes intention. And intention yields five benefits.

Intentions Keep You Focused Intentions keep you from getting lost in the busyness of life. Intentions prevent you from driving in circles by pointing you in the right direction. If you get off track, intentions will speak to you in a polite manner and remind you when you need to turn around: "I'm not enjoying my daughter, I'm stressed about her homework. Maybe we could first get some frozen yogurt after school tomorrow instead of me jumping on her about the homework."

Intentions Keep You Centered Intentions keep you centered in the middle of the adolescent storm. They also keep you centered with your busy schedules. Instead of feeling scattered, intentions bring you back to what's important to you. When you are centered, the cortical and subcortical parts of your brain integrate so you can think clearly (remember Chapter 2?). Your whole self comes together. All the different parts come into alignment: your thoughts, actions, feelings, behavior, values, beliefs, and spirituality. This allows you to be fully present to your daughter and your life.

Intentions Remind You of What's Important You need constant reminders to keep yourself on track. Your kids and everything else can be distractions. As I was working on this chapter and set an intention about my writing, I got a "mom help" text from my daughter, after which my dog was limping so badly I had to take her to the vet. Everything turned out fine, but I needed my intention to remind me to get back to work.

Because life has a way of interrupting, it's good to put your intention in writing so you can remember it day after day. You can write your intention on an index card, sticky note, or place it on the screen saver on your phone. The point is to keep it visible so it's always in the forefront of your mind.

Intentions Rewire Your Brain Human beings have a propensity to go to the negative. We also tend to default to the same old thoughts, feelings, and behaviors. Another way to say this is that we tend to remember our negative ways and forget our new positive intentions. This is why many of us get discouraged and give up. The good news is that your brain can be rewired. Remembering your intention rewires your brain to go toward what you want instead of what you don't want.

Intentions Redirect Your Attention   Intentions redirect your attention to what you want. Rather than looking for evidence of why your life won't change, your attention looks for evidence of why it can. If your intention is to enjoy your teenage daughter, then your attention begins thinking of ways that can happen. "I'm always on my daughter's back. I need to spend some downtime with my daughter. We could watch an episode on Netflix, or go out to breakfast."

Three Practical Ways to Use Intentions

There are many ways you can use intentions. Three practical ways you can use them in your daily life are in focusing on the big picture, having your intention be a driving question, and realizing that you have specific intentions for different situations. Big picture intentions act like a compass and keep you moving in the right direction. Driving questions help your actions stay aligned with your intentions. Specific intentions help you be your best self in your day-to-day interactions.

Focus on the Big Picture   You don't want to get overwhelmed with too many intentions. Start with one "big picture intention," such as "I intend to enjoy my daughter in this last year of high school." Big picture intentions are not short-term intentions ("I intend to have a good time at the beach with my daughter tomorrow") because they involve changing behavior over the long term. You can create a big picture intention for a season of time like the summer or school year.

To create your big picture intention:

- Start your intention with "I intend to_____." Avoid tentative words like "hope," "maybe," "try," or "want to."

- Use your intention as a guiding principle. "I intend to vacuum" is not an intention. An intention is not an item on a to-do list.

- Ask yourself, "What do I really, really want to change but am afraid I won't be successful at it?" For example:

  - If you're afraid that you will give in or lose it with your daughter, your intention is "I intend to be strong, calm, and clear with my daughter."

  - If you're afraid you are going to be constantly stressed, your intention is "I intend to slow down and enjoy my life."

  - If you're sick of all the drama with your daughter, and you're afraid it will never end, your intention is "I intend to be at peace with myself and my daughter."

  - If you're tired of that low-level job, and you're afraid you're unqualified for something more interesting and better paying, your intention is "I intend to go back to school to finish my degree."

Turn Your Intention into a Driving Question All day long we ask ourselves questions. We do this in the mental chatter of our minds. Most of the time we're not aware of it. These questions are repetitive and automatic and are not helpful at all. "Why can't you get it together?" "Why are you so stupid?" "Why does everyone think they can walk all over me?" These automatic questions come from the Sneaky Mean Voice and make it hard to move forward.

You can replace automatic questions with an intentional question, and then use the answers to drive your actions. You do this simply, by turning your intention into a question. For example, take the intention, "I intend to enjoy my daughter today." The intentional question would be, "How can I enjoy my daughter today?"

Intentional questions get you back on track because they redirect your attention and imagination. They also lead you to a practical answer. When you ask yourself, "How can I enjoy my daughter today?" the answer is specific. "I'm going to go to my daughter's room and just hang out with her and the new puppy. I will wait an hour before I ask her about her homework."

Create Specific Intentions for Different Situations You likely have intentions for different situations, though you may not call them "intentions." If you're hosting a dinner party, you want people to feel comfortable and welcome in your home. You put a lot of energy into creating an atmosphere that will allow this to happen. If you're speaking in front of a group, you want to be relaxed, confident, and engaging. You may feel tired before you get on stage, but you put on your best self and present with enthusiasm.

The problem is that when you are home, you want to relax. You let your guard down and are internally unprepared for what's about to hit you. Specific intentions can help you with this.

If I asked you when the most stressful times with your daughter are, I bet you would know. It would be before or after school. It would be right before a test, final, tryout, audition, or college application. It would be when your daughter's best friend betrayed her or her boyfriend broke her heart. In other words, your most stressful times are whenever your daughter is stressed. If you know when your daughter is going to be stressed and you know how she's going to act, why walk blindly into the drama trap? Yet most mothers do this. They fall into the same traps over and over, and still feel blindsided.

Setting a specific intention for a specific stressful situation is a game changer. Anticipating how your daughter is going to act helps you get internally prepared. Then you can decide how you will show up and what you will do. You do this through your intention. A specific intention like, "I intend to stay centered and calm when my daughter comes home from school," reminds you who you choose to be, no matter how your daughter is feeling when she walks in.

* * *

Many mothers find themselves in Mother Fog because they constantly respond to the needs around them and lose their center. You don't have to live that way. Remember, clarity beats fog every time. You can't parent effectively without clarity—and effective parenting eliminates a plethora of drama.

Your clarity is a process, and you don't get there overnight. First identify where you are and what's not working. Then, with courage and faith, take the next step and identify what you want. Turn this clarity into intention. Your intention gives you the resolve and determination to get you to where you want to go.

CHAPTER 5

How to Reclaim Your "I Feel Good" Energy

You would love Cindy. She's bright, intelligent, has a great sense of humor, and owns her own business, a counseling center for women. Cindy is married and has a seventeen-year-old son, Mike, and a thirteen-year-old daughter, Addison. "Mike is easy, but Addison is another story," Cindy said. "I hope to God I can make it through these teenage years."

Cindy was tired from having to stay on top of Addison for several hours every evening to get her to do her homework. The hardest part was all the mean things Addison would say. "After all I do for Addison . . . ," Cindy continued. "I make sure she has private lessons with the best gymnastic instructors. I take her shopping. I'll take her with me to get a manicure. I'm always going to the store for her. After all that, she says she hates me. She says I'm the worst mother in the world, and tells me to get out of her life."

Cindy felt betrayed and hurt. She had sacrificed so much for Addison, and it was starting to affect other areas of her life. She admitted that she was no longer enjoying her work, she was having more arguments with her husband, and it felt like forever since she'd seen her friends. Bottom line, Cindy was exhausted and not enjoying any part of her life.

Cindy signed up for my parenting program, where she learned that mothers are good at pouring out their "I feel good" energy to their family and communities, but not good at replenishing this energy for themselves. When *good energy*—short for "I feel good" energy—is used up, moms are left with "I feel terrible and resent my life" energy.

Why a Mother's Life Is Like a Cup

I explained to Cindy that a mother's life is like a cup: whatever is in the cup is poured out to the family. If mom feels happy and fulfilled, she pours out her joy to her family. I call this the Cup of Blessings. If, on the other hand, mom feels exhausted and irritated, she pours out her frustration instead. I call this the Cup of Overwhelmed. When mothers parent from the Cup of Blessings, everyone wins; when they parent from the Cup of Overwhelmed, everyone loses.

Cindy admitted that she was parenting from the Cup of Overwhelmed. I told her that she could switch to parenting from the Cup of Blessings, but that she first had to reclaim her good energy. This begins with believing Powerful Parenting Message #1, "It's crucial to pay attention to me."

After the third week of my program, I asked Cindy how things were going. "Great!" she told me. "I took time off from work and went to lunch with friends. I went and saw a movie by myself and loved it." When she also told me she hadn't done much for her daughter, I challenged her on this. "Taking care of yourself is doing something for your daughter," I said. "Come to think about it, you're right," Cindy responded. "She got upset at me the other night, but I forgot about it. I handled the situation and got Addison on track. I was in such a good mood, it didn't get to me."

The Cycle of Blessings

Maintaining your energy level so that you have something positive to give your family while still retaining your good energy involves The Cycle of Blessings, as illustrated below. The cycle begins with being "Blessed," by which I mean that you are filled with joy, peace, compassion, kindness, patience, strength, creativity, and love. You are filled with good energy. In this state, you are naturally grateful for the things in your life, and see the beauty in the world. Your life is the Cup of Blessings and, because your life is brimming with good things, you want to give to your family and it comes easy. There is no resentment; instead, you get a satisfaction from taking care of your family.

When you pour out your blessings, it matters greatly what's in your cup. You may do the same things for your family that you've always done, but when you have the wrong attitude, the blessing is soured. What's inside you is evident in your words and actions. Statements like, "I could have spent money on clothes for me but instead I bought you a formal dress," or "You better treat me with respect or I'm not doing anything nice for you again" are loaded with threats, cynicism, and stress, and clearly have strings attached. You must give because you *want* to. Your daughter can tell the difference. She feels nurtured, loved, and taken care of when you say things like, "I found a great dress for next Friday's dance when I was at Macy's. It's exactly the color and style you love."

The final step is to replenish the blessings. Another way to say it is that you are replenishing your good energy. The problem is that some moms try to skip this step. We are not an unending fountain of blessings, so when we pour out our good energy, it will run out if we don't replenish.

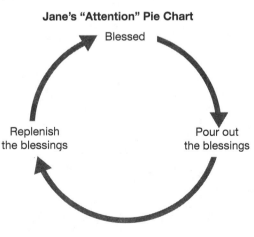

Jane's "Attention" Pie Chart

Blessed

Replenish the blessings

Pour out the blessings

Although your good energy has run out, your cup is not empty. Your Cup of Blessings morphs into the Cup of Overwhelmed and is full of negative energy. You are going to give what is inside of your cup. If you are completely overwhelmed, you give overwhelmed. If you are frustrated you give frustration. You get the idea. When you become the Cup of Overwhelmed, it doesn't mean that you are a bad mom; it means that you haven't replenished the blessings. Let's compare the Cup of Blessings with the Cup of Overwhelmed.

Cup of Blessings	Cup of Overwhelmed
You are full of gratitude and appreciation.	You constantly complain and whine.
It would take a huge event for you to lose it.	One word can make you blow a gasket.
Everyone wins.	No one wins.
You are reflective and self-aware.	You are disconnected from yourself.
You have clear intentions.	You are confused and reactive.
You say yes from your true self.	You say yes to please everyone but yourself.
You have your needed rest and downtime.	You are running 24/7.
You give out of joy.	You give out of obligation.
You are energized by your life's work.	You dread your busywork and to-do lists.

No mom wants to be the Cup of Overwhelmed; you end up there by default. This is what happened to my client Mercedes, the mother of a six-, nine-, and fourteen-year-old, who works full-time and has a husband who travels during the week (so not much help there). It had been a month since I had seen Mercedes in my office, and when I saw her again she looked exhausted. She had been out of town twice in the past month for work, and when traveling she didn't get enough sleep because of meetings from morning to night. Then, when Mercedes returned home, she hit the ground running with work and family.

"I'm not doing well," Mercedes told me. She went on to explain that she had been drinking way too much wine, and would then binge on food and blow off her exercise. Then, the night before our session, she had raged at her fourteen-year-old daughter. In tears, she told me she wanted to leave town again and get away from the kids.

This was not a bad mother. It was an exhausted mother who had been depleted of all her good energy. It hadn't even crossed her mind to replenish her blessings.

What Drains Your Good Energy?

The greatest number of comments I have ever received on my Facebook page came from two questions: "What is the #1 drain in your life? What is the biggest drain on your energy?" It turns out that moms have quite a lot to say about feeling drained, and that most of them feel powerless to change it. Here are a couple of comments they shared:

> *"I'm drained because I don't do anything for myself, and don't even know what I would like to do for myself. Instead, I spend every day doing for others . . . cooking, cleaning, lunches, laundry, and working a full-time job."*

> *"I'm drained because there's no time for me. I work all day, come home to encounter a sink full of dirty dishes, dirty clothes, and a teen girl upstairs on 'face time' with friends who can't even say hello! I feel like I'm taken for granted."*

There are many reasons that moms feel drained. First, feeling drained is normal. If you pour out your good energy to your family, it's only natural you will feel drained.

Feeling Drained Is Normal

If you want to feel good about yourself, write down everything you do in one week. I think you'll be surprised by how much you do. It will become evident why you feel exhausted and drained of energy. There are many facets to your life, but let's just focus on how much energy it takes to parent your teenage daughter:

- **You nurture her.** You hold and comfort your daughter when her best friend betrays her.

- **You give her guidance.** You help her think through how she will get her homework done.

- **You encourage her.** You remind her of how far she has come, and tell her not to give up simply because she didn't get the part in the school play.

- **You monitor her behavior.** You make sure she gets up on time, gets her homework done, and gets to bed at a reasonable hour.

- **You protect her.** You make sure that parents will be at the party she will attend.

- **You set limits.** You take your thirteen-year-old daughter's iPhone when she goes to bed.

- **You invest your physical energy.** You shuttle her around to soccer practice after school. You cook, clean, and run to the store to buy a book for her English class.

- **You make time for her.** You relax in her room, talking, listening to her music (!!), or looking through magazines.

As you can see, your daughter takes a significant amount of your energy—and this is without the drama! Add in a little drama and stress to everything else in your life, and, yes, it is normal to feel drained.

The Combo Effect A common pitfall that leaves you exhausted, stressed, and overwhelmed is what I call the "combo effect." There are so many moving pieces in your life—a child or children, a spouse, extended family, work, friends, maintaining a home—that while these are all good things and worthy of your time, each component seems doable until you combine them, at which point they equal way too much.

It's easy to underestimate how that *one more thing* will impact your life. When you say yes to the *one more thing,* the scales get tipped from a full rewarding life to an overcommitted, chaotic one. Imagine this.

Your daughter has homecoming this week. This means she needs a dress, shoes, and a haircut. You also have a project due at work and you need to put in extra hours. Your friend calls and needs to talk *now.* Your husband tells you that his mother is coming to visit this weekend. All of this together equals one stressed-out mom.

These kinds of scenarios happen all the time. Something similar happened to Lashonda, one of my clients. She came to my office looking distraught and said it was a horrible week. The *one more thing* was that her mother came uninvited to her thirteen-year-old daughter's birthday party. Her mother is a difficult person, and is not much help. Lashonda got so stressed, she wrecked her car backing out of the driveway, and ended up yelling at the birthday girl just before the party started. Lashonda felt there was something wrong with her for not being able to handle things better. But it wasn't her fault. It was the combo effect.

There are numerous demands on you and it's challenging getting through the list. If you can't get it done, you're not a failure. This is a scheduling problem (which I address in Chapter 11). It's simple math. You have a certain amount of energy and there are limited hours in a day. You just don't have enough energy or hours in the day to get everything done.

Life's Interruptions Life doesn't always run smoothly. There are factors that are unpredictable and that unexpectedly invade your life. This is especially true when raising a teenage daughter.

This morning I had set aside time to write, when my daughter called and told me she had two flat tires on the way to her finals. It wasn't anyone's fault, but it was still stressful and threw my schedule off.

Then there are the hard things in life: the unexpected divorce, losing a friend to cancer, a car accident, the loss of job, a natural disaster, or the death of a parent. These unwanted visitors will take a toll on your body, soul, mind, and spirit. This is a normal reaction to trauma, but too many moms add shame to the mix. They think there's something wrong with them if they can't keep up the pace. During these times you need to be extremely kind to yourself and replenish your blessings.

Decreasing or Removing Those Unnecessary Major Drains

There are many kinds of drains on our good energy. Some of them, like a flat tire (your own or your daughter's) are relatively minor. Others, such as finding out that your sister has breast cancer are major indeed. And, as we learned above, events and moments that you would ordinarily take in stride can come at just the wrong time—or in the wrong combination—and blow you out of the water.

Often, however, the most disheartening drains on our energy or time are unnecessary. But unlike life's interruptions, we can do something about them; they are of our own making. With attention, strategy, and support, we can significantly decrease the drains or remove them completely. Take the example of the messy house. You can get your house in order and eliminate that drain, without a doubt. However, there are other factors that make it difficult.

Have you ever noticed that when the dirty dishes in the sink are yours, they are tolerable, but when they are your daughter's or your spouse's dishes, this can really get under your skin—especially when it happens day after day, and year after year. Now the drain is much bigger than a messy house.

Here's why. The meaning you attribute to why your family has messed up your house is going to make it either a major or minor drain. If the meaning is "I don't matter. My family takes me for granted. I'm being used," it's going to be major. Those thoughts are incredibly draining, and there is a good chance they aren't even true. The problem is that if you *believe* it's true, then every pair of shoes tossed on the floor means your family doesn't care about you. These types of thoughts disempower you and lead to feelings of resignation.

You eliminate this drain by changing the meaning from major to minor. Instead of interpreting this as a personal attack, consider that perhaps the reason the shoes are scattered on the floor is that you have a messy family, especially the ten-year-old. Pretty minor, don't you think? Now you can bring the attention back to what you want. What does a clean and organized house mean to you? Why is it important to you? When you are clear about this, what you can do to change it will become clear.

Another unnecessary major drain is drama with your daughter and anyone else in your life. This too becomes a major drain because of how you interpret or handle it. Is the drama a personal attack on you or is it that she's a work in progress? How you answer this question will determine how major or minor these dramas will be. This is an important issue that I discuss in Chapter 7.

How to Reclaim Your Good Energy

I saw Brianna last week and she looked great. "I forgot what it felt like to feel good," she told me, her face beaming. This made my day. Brianna had come so far since her gut-wrenching divorce a year earlier. Her husband, Wendell, was an emotionally abusive alcoholic and had embezzled money from her business. The fallout from his actions had crushed their fourteen-year-old daughter, Jasmine, causing her grades to fall and confidence to drop.

For the past year, Brianna had to deal with lawyers, accountants, an angry ex-husband, as well as a horrific amount of money owed in back taxes. She was afraid of what her ex-husband might do to her, she was scared she could lose her house and her business, and she worried about how all of this would affect Jasmine. Brianna's self-worth was shaken, but the hardest part for her to deal with was her lack of energy.

Brianna was willing to do what it takes to feel good again. She worked with a personal trainer three times a week, changed her diet, and surrounded herself with upbeat friends. With more energy, she made positive changes at work, including hiring a talented office manager, and her business started to pick up. As her life continued to turn around, Brianna kept trying new things. She went on a yoga retreat, took a cooking class, started playing piano again, and even went contradancing. "I felt like someone turned back the clock. I almost feel like a kid again," Brianna said. "I think what made these changes possible is that I began valuing *me* again. I know I have a higher purpose and I want to give back. My daughter used to worry about me, but not anymore."

Brianna used her unexpected divorce as a catalyst to get her good energy back. It doesn't have to take a traumatic event; you can decide now to reclaim your good energy. It starts with giving yourself permission.

Give Yourself Permission to Feel Good Again

Permission begins with remembering the Powerful Parenting Message #1, "It's crucial to pay attention to me." Fundamental to this permission is that you value your whole self. This is what Brianna realized. Valuing, rather than belittling, herself was the key to feeling good again.

You have to claim your right to feel good again; you can't wait for anyone else to give you permission. I've heard this a thousand times when working with couples in my private practice. The wife is angry with her husband because he went to the gym, played golf, went cycling, or had a beer with some friends. But he hasn't done anything wrong. He has given himself permission to refuel, as the wife could have—and let me say "should have"—done. I tell my moms that they need to claim their right to feel good again.

Take 100 Percent Responsibility for Your Life To reclaim your "I Feel Good" energy, you have to take full responsibility for your life. This means having to let go of your excuses. It's easy to blame any dissatisfaction in your life on your daughter, partner, boss, or parents. It would have been easy for Brianna to play the victim card because her husband betrayed her again and again. She could have complained to anyone and everyone, but she would not have gotten what she really wanted—which was to feel good again.

Taking responsibility for your life means committing to decrease or remove the unnecessary drains in your life. It starts with your decision to get the support and help needed to remove the unnecessary major drains. Brianna was able to move out of a draining and abusive situation because she sought out social, spiritual, psychological, legal, and professional support.

Be the Guardian of Your Soul To take this deeper, you must be the guardian of your soul. By soul, I mean that deep, inner, sacred part of you. It's what connects you to intuition, wisdom, creativity, and God. It's where you hold space for those you truly love. It's the part of you that can love unconditionally, rise from the ashes, and move forward with optimism. The soul is the gateway for feeling energized and alive again.

You can't parent effectively if your soul is wounded. You may call this losing hope or confidence, but the result is the same: You begin to feel dead inside.

Being the guardian of your soul does not mean that no one else can look out for you or protect you. But it does mean that you must be your own advocate by saying no to the *one more thing*, removing yourself from negative situations, changing your interpretation of or attitude toward circumstances, and protecting your heart. Because if you don't, your very essence will diminish.

Know What Replenishes You

It's important to be aware of what truly replenishes you. Here's why. When your body is low on good energy, it protests. Unconsciously you feel, "I deserve some reward. This isn't fair. I'm not having any fun. I hate how I feel." On automatic pilot, you will grab anything to feel good. This is not a well-thought-out-plan, it's a gut reaction, and it will not replenish your good energy. What it does is temporarily numb your bad feelings.

The Problem with Numbing Your Negative Feelings When you numb the negative feelings, you also numb the positive ones. Numbing is not a solution, it's a temporary fix. You numb in proportion to how bad or irritating your day was.

When you've had a terrible day . . .

- You eat a big bag of chips or finish the half-gallon of ice cream.

- You pour yourself a glass of wine and, before you know it, you have emptied the bottle.

- You sit in front of the TV for hours or spend way too much time looking at Facebook.

- You go shopping and buy four pairs of shoes that you don't need.

As you can see, numbing doesn't work. It creates a whole new set of problems and depletes you even more. You gain weight, wake up with a hangover, feel like you don't have a life, and throw away your money. It doesn't make you feel any better. At best, you'll feel blah. Most often it adds shame to the mix. Now you feel worse because you ate, drank, or spent too much.

Be Intentional by Knowing What You Want for Your Life To reclaim your good energy you have to be intentional. It's not going to happen naturally. You have to decide that this is what you really want for your life. To do this, you need to be clear. First, do you know what gives you that good energy or makes your soul come alive? This is not a cookie-cutter formula; it's specific to your own preferences and likes.

I asked several moms what gave them "I feel good" energy, they said . . .

- Taking a nap

- Having time to write in their journals and pray

- Remembering their purpose

- Making a gratitude list and focusing on what's going right

- Getting out in nature and watching the sunset

- Running, or some other kind of exercise

- Having lunch with a good friend

- Relaxing at home watching movies with their family

- Dancing, museums, and jet skiing

- A night of listening to jazz

Now it's your turn. Answer the following six questions.

1. What gives me "I feel good" energy is_____.

2. I feel the most alive when _____.

3. What helps me relax is _____.

4. I feel like myself when _____.

5. What nourishes my soul is _____.

6. I'm proud of myself when _____.

If this exercise feels hard to you, don't worry. You're not alone. Many moms are so focused on their families that they don't know how to take care of themselves.

Revisiting the Five Essential Needs for Feeling Good

Finally, let's conclude this chapter by revisiting the five essential needs for feeling good discussed on pages 21–27 in Chapter 1 from the perspective of reclaiming your "I feel good" energy.

Foundational Needs

Taking good care of your physical body is foundational for your good energy. You feel good when you get plenty of sleep, have downtime and relax, eat healthy meals, and exercise consistently.

Maintenance Needs

The maintenance of your personal life and family life is critical to your good energy. You feel good when your home is decorated the way you like it, everything is in order, your papers are filed, and the clutter is gone. You feel good when your car is cleaned and vacuumed. You feel good when you like the clothes you wear.

Relational Needs

Feeling loved and appreciated fills you with good energy. You feel good when you are relaxed and enjoying quality time with your family and friends. You feel good when you watch movies, play with your dog, go to the beach, and enjoy a long leisurely meal with a loved one. It feels good when you can be yourself and still be accepted, loved, and valued.

Personal Enrichment Needs

Mothers frequently dismiss this need because it feels frivolous. At first glance, it seems to benefit you and not your family. Nothing can be further from the truth. Personal-enrichment is the quickest way to get your spark back, and to find fulfillment and purpose in life. This is backed by science. Novel experiences increase the positive brain chemicals like serotonin. This is why it feels good to express your creativity, take a dance class or piano lesson, or redecorate your home. You feel good when you challenge yourself physically, whether this means running on a treadmill or your first marathon. You feel good leaving a routine, boring job and finding work that is meaningful and rewarding. You feel good when you travel and learn about other cultures.

Spiritual Needs

What better way to refill your good energy than by tapping into the source of all life and energy? You do this through prayer, meditation, inspirational reading, reflection, gratitude, worship, and basking in the beauty of nature. All of these things facilitate an intimate connection with God.

You feel good when you are in alignment with God. You feel good when you drink in the beauty of a sunset. You feel good when you are filled with love and compassion for the world. You feel good when you can reflect on all the serendipitous moments in your day. You feel good when you know you are making positive contributions to the world, no matter how small (even if you are just being kind to the cashier at the grocery store).

Start reclaiming your "I Feel Good" energy today. Download your Five Essential Needs for Feeling Good Worksheet at www.colleen ogrady.com/bookresources.

* * *

It takes a lot to parent a teenage daughter while dealing with everything else in your life. Moms are good at pouring out their "I Feel Good" energy but fall short on reclaiming it. That's why it's important to understand the Cycle of Blessings. Feeling drained is normal, but with attention and strategy you can decrease or remove those unnecessary major drains that drag you down. To reclaim your good energy, get clear about what energizes you; it could be as simple as taking a nap, watching the sunset, or having dinner with your daughter. Or start something new, like a blog, or plan a moms' getaway weekend with a few good friends. Keeping the five essential needs in mind as a framework will help you identify various ways you can refuel.

PART II

Rebuilding Your Connection with Your Daughter

CHAPTER 6

How to Like Your Daughter Again

It was a Thursday evening, a week after Thanksgiving, but Andrea and her daughter Natalie were far from thankful. Natalie, a junior in high school, was tightly wrapped in a blanket on my sofa. Her mother sat cross-legged next to her. It was clear that Natalie was hurt and that Andrea was angry. "It's not working. I can't take this anymore" Andrea said. "I'm just waiting till she graduates and is out of this house." Natalie was crying at this point and looking down. "Natalie wouldn't get up this morning, so I kicked her," Andrea continued. I was stunned. She said it matter-of-factly and with no apology. "I was hoping Natalie and I would have a good relationship, but it's not possible." Natalie had now shut down completely, so I asked her mom if I could speak to her alone. Natalie told me that Mom had come into her room yelling at her to get up and they needed to leave for school in twenty minutes. "Yes, she pissed me off," Natalie told me, "and I wasn't going to get out of bed after she yelled at me, but then Mom kicked me three times. I didn't even touch her. She thinks I'm such a terrible kid, but I am making all A's except in Algebra. You heard her. She can't wait till I'm gone. She wonders why I am so unhappy."

This was neither a horrible mother nor daughter, but they had fallen into the downward cycle of drama. Andrea regretted her life as a teenager, when she didn't make good grades and got pregnant in high school. She was doing everything she could to prevent Natalie from making the same mistakes. The problem was that her relationship with Natalie had been reduced to checking and monitoring her behavior 24/7. If this is all you have in your relationship with your daughter, you are not going to like her very much and she *certainly* won't like you.

It's common for moms to worry, obsess, and do their best to love their daughters. But it's hard to like someone who disrespects you and makes you feel like a failure.

If this rings true for you, don't give up yet! I've been there. When my daughter was twelve, I, of course, loved her, but it was hard to like her and she probably felt the same way about me. I knew there had to be a way to connect.

As I write this book, my daughter is in her senior year of high school. A few weeks ago, I came home from work and she said, "Mom, come look at these YouTube videos." Now what I really wanted to do was change out of my work clothes and relax, but I walked over to her and sat down. I was expecting some teen video (that I wasn't going to be thrilled about), but instead she played a video of Josh Groban. In the video, he singled out this plain-looking woman in the audience to sing a duet with him, and she happened to have an amazing voice. I told my daughter, "That goes on my bucket list." She looked at me with a mischievous grin and said, "He's going to be here next week."

Before I knew it, my daughter had found two tickets in the second row. (Of course, I would have picked out tickets in the very back.) I told her that I had to see clients that night, but she said, "You just said this was on your bucket list." I realized this was one of those magic moments. My daughter will be leaving for college soon. When does your teen ask you to go to a concert with her? And I really do like Josh Groban. So I said, "Let's do it" and canceled my clients. The concert was amazing, and my daughter kept looking at me during the concert with a gleam in her eye and said, "See, aren't you glad I made you go?"

Actually I was very glad, and it was a magical night that my daughter and I will never forget. The pleasure we shared erased any tiny guilt I may have felt about canceling my clients. We still smile at each other every time we hear the phrase "bucket list."

Positive experiences small or large really help with the "like" factor. I really like my daughter. That's why it made me sad for Andrea and Natalie. Not all experiences with my daughter are fabulous. There is going to be tension if I am doing my job as a mom. Because teens have an undeveloped prefrontal cortex, they are like a car with faulty brakes. There are times I need to step in and put the *brakes on* when a fun opportunity arises and my daughter has not considered the consequences.

But through the principles and tools in this chapter, I turned my relationship with my daughter around, and I've helped hundreds of mothers and daughters in my practice and programs—including Andrea and Natalie—do the same. And you can too!

Don't Give Up on a Healthy Relationship with Your Teenage Daughter

Many of you are grieving the loss of your Disney princess. You may feel as if she has been invaded by a defiant alien. But your little girl still exists. She's buried under teenage bravado and antics, but every once in a while, you will catch a glimpse of her—especially if you'll embrace the suggestions we'll get to in a moment.

At this point you may be thinking, "Is it even possible to have a good relationship with my teenage daughter?" Absolutely! I don't mean twenty-four hours a day, but you will be able to find pockets of connection and joy every day. Sometimes they come in ordinary life exchanges and sometimes they are bigger experiences. But it's going to look different from any other relationship. You need a different set of criteria and expectations to evaluate a relationship with a teenager.

"What does a healthy relationship with my teenage daughter look like?" you ask. This is the million-dollar question, because it's complicated on several levels. If the relationship feels confusing, it's not just you. It's difficult because of where your daughter is, both developmentally and emotionally. And it's hard, because relational tension is a perfectly normal part of the mother–daughter relationship.

There are huge developmental changes happening in your teenage daughter. Teenage girls are supposed to strive for more autonomy and independence. It's normal for teenage girls to be less dependent on parents and more detached. This can be confusing, because your daughter is on a continuum between dependence on you and increasing independence. Sometimes she begs for your attention, and other times she acts as if she doesn't know you. It's easy to see why moms get confused and hurt.

Your daughter's emotions are all over the place. Understanding her physiological development will be helpful here (we'll talk more about this in the next chapter). One morning she plops on your bed telling you lots of stories. Thirty minutes later she slams the door and wants to be alone. Two hours later, she passes you in the kitchen and says, "Hey, Mom," as if nothing ever happened. It's no wonder you don't know where you stand!

Though she looks like an adult, your daughter needs your guidance more than ever. If you're doing your job as a parent, there's going to be tension. Your job is to protect her and provide structure for her. She has to comply with your rules and, when she doesn't, there have to be consequences. You have the power and money, and she doesn't, which sets you up as the adversary. At the same time, she is growing in her maturity and responsibility and is supposed to push for more independence. Sounds like tension to me.

But despite all of these challenges, it is possible and crucial to have a healthy relationship with your daughter through her teenage years. Even though she is depending on her friends more and developing her autonomy, a secure attachment with your daughter matters significantly. An article by Marlene M. Moretti and Maya Peled in the October 2004 issue of *Paediatric Child Health* confirms that a healthy connection between a parent and teen is linked to better perform-ance and coping strategies, and more competence in peer relation-ships. A healthy connection is correlated with fewer mental health problems such as anxiety, depression, conduct disorder, delinquency, and aggression. The research also showed lower rates of teenage preg-nancy, eating disorders, excessive drinking, drug use, and risky sexual behavior.

Yes, a healthy relationship with your daughter is attainable and im-portant, and there are three elements that make a secure connection:

- Being there for your daughter

- Being tuned in

- Being responsive

Let's explore each of these elements.

Being There for Your Daughter

You provide the secure foundation for your daughter in the rough seas of adolescence. When your daughter is being tossed by the waves of stress, peer pressure, hormones, and self- doubt, you are her anchor. You stay grounded and unmovable when the waves of drama hit. Your relationship with your daughter is the rope that connects her to you. Despite her erratic behavior and wildly varying emotions, your sta-bility provides the secure attachment. Later, when she is ready, she can sail off on her own—and you can rest easy in the knowledge that you have helped her develop a sturdy rudder to steer with.

Your daughter will never be *your* anchor of stability, though. She can be there for you in limited ways. She can be thoughtful and help-ful. Listen to your stories. Have good manners and show respect. Give you cards and presents. But her moods are all over the place, and this is normal developmentally. You are the parent and she is the child, not your best friend. Yes, you can have a deep connection with her, but she can't meet your emotional needs. When your daughter is a teenager, she's not at an age when you can lean on her or when she can give you support. This is why, going back to the power-filled messages we discussed earlier, it's crucial that you pay attention to *you*—your daughter can't do it.

Being available to your daughter means you are available for her to touch base with you periodically. It does *not* mean:

- You are glued to her side.

- You are in her room watching her text her friends.

- You go to the movies with her every weekend.

- You talk her ear off.

- You don't have a life.

Remember, she is somewhere on the continuum between dependency and autonomy. One minute she talks your ear off, and the next she hides in her girl cave. This approach/distance dance can drive you nuts. But when your daughter needs space, don't take it personally. It's easy to confuse this as rejection, but it's what healthy teenage girls do. It's not about you, it's about her developing autonomy. If you take it as rejection, you're going to react by getting angry or withdrawing from her.

She will open up to you, but only sporadically. When your daughter is relaxed, she will touch base with you, sharing the ordinary things that happen during the day. "Touching base" is not an intense conversation about feelings; what she shares with you may seem completely insignificant and ridiculous, like looking at silly pictures on her phone. But when you take the time to interact with her world, even at the frivolous level, she feels connected to you. It may seem like nothing, but she gets the message that she matters.

Here's what touching base looks like in my house. I pick my daughter up from school. Sometimes she's very chatty, and sometimes she's not. If she's not, I don't push her. When we get home, she goes straight to her room and checks her messages. If I leave her alone, she usually comes into my room and plops on my bed and tells me about her day.

Sometimes she's grumpy after school and needs to eat. I leave her alone. Then later, she finds me in the house and invites me to watch a show on TV or spontaneously tells me something about school.

Think of it this way. Your daughter is like a cat. You can't tell your cat to come to you. The more forceful your approach to your cat, the more she runs away and hides. But when you chill out on the sofa, the cat jumps up and nuzzles up to you. Just like a cat, your daughter is going to bolt if you try to force the conversation.

Believe me, I learned this the hard way. Let's just say my daughter is not a morning person, but when she was in seventh grade I didn't get the message. I'm a working mom and like to be efficient with my time. It made sense to me that driving to school was a great time to check in and connect with my daughter. I would ask her questions like, "Did you remember your homework?" or "How do you feel about your math test?"

Her reaction was as predictable as putting your hand on a hot stove. She would blow up and say disrespectful things. Then I would respond with a long-winded lecture. Our "bonding time" ended with her leaping out of the car and slamming the car door. Of course, every mother loves her daughter, but after those kinds of interactions, the "like" meter plummets into the red zone.

Then I noticed that when I wasn't trying to force a conversation, she would spontaneously initiate one. It seemed like out of the blue, my daughter would grab our two dogs and pounce on my bed. She would tell me every juicy detail about her day, who she hung out with and what boy she had a crush on. She would show me videos on YouTube. We would laugh at our dogs. But there was a catch. The time wasn't convenient to me.

I was usually on my computer. I was tempted to say, "Sorry, you missed your chance this morning." But then it hit me: in the mornings she was stressed and sleepy. She was gearing up for school like a soldier gearing up for war. When my daughter was relaxed, she was ready to connect. I realized then that these spontaneous conversations were worth everything—and were much more important than my self-imposed schedule. They put the "like" back into our relationship, and they built a bridge of connection that protects her in times of crises.

I often hear moms say, "My daughter won't talk to me." She *will* talk to you but you may need to change your approach. It's important to evaluate how you try to talk to your daughter. If all your communication is monitoring her behavior, checking up on her, and pressuring her to talk, she is going to be guarded or reactive. This is where spontaneous conversations can help. In a spontaneous conversation you have no agenda other than enjoying your daughter.

Spontaneous conversations begin in the shallow waters. She tells you something "really stupid" her teacher said. This may not be interesting to you, but you need to meet her where she is. You want your daughter talking to you in an easy and relaxed way.

Often, moms dismiss spontaneous conversations as unimportant. They think, "Of course she'll talk to me when it's about something that doesn't matter, but when I try to talk about her grades she won't say a word."

Even the things we think are goofy and insignificant are important to her. She has to trust you with the little things before she lets you into the bigger things. Trust me, if you start out in the shallow waters, she will go in the deep waters with you.

I supervised psychiatry residents in a medical school for nineteen years. I observed beginning residents behind a two-way mirror. One resident I supervised was having his first session with Beth, a sixteen-year-old girl. Beth had just been discharged from a psychiatric hospital for a suicide attempt.

I instructed the resident to start with a neutral question like, "Do you play sports?" But during the first session, the resident got nervous and the first thing he asked her was, "Do you have any suicidal ideations?" (a typical psychiatry question). At that point, Beth shut down and wouldn't talk to him.

The psychiatry resident needed help. I went in the room and asked Beth what she liked to do for fun. She told me she liked to play volleyball. I asked her more questions about volleyball. She let down her guard and told me what she loved about the game and bragged about her "mean" serve. Because Beth was relaxed, she started talking spontaneously. Fifteen minutes later she brought up the suicide attempt and told me why she would never try it again. Only when she felt relaxed and safe could she open up.

What worked with Beth will work with your daughter. Let your daughter initiate the conversation and talk about something that she's comfortable with. The bonus is that she'll leak out more information when she's relaxed. Speaking casually together can lead to your daughter sharing her true feelings about her boyfriend. When you don't force it, the conversation naturally evolves.

The Benefits of Spontaneous Conversations

It's tempting to think that your daughter is wasting your time when she approaches you with something that appears trivial. You feel the pressure to get through your list, like getting the dinner started, or paying the bills. But hidden in the spontaneous conversations is pure gold, and you don't want to miss these benefits.

- **Spontaneous conversations make good deposits in your daughter's emotional bank.** Filling up her emotional bank with good experiences strengthens your relationship because she experiences your care, comfort, interest, approval, and delight.

- **Spontaneous conversations help get you through the bad times.** If your daughter's overall experiences with you are positive, your relationship will bounce back quicker after a disagreement. She may be mad at you, but she will be more motivated to repair the relationship. Without communication, your connection will be strained, so when you are in a disagreement, she will be more likely to react and rebel and in general throw an extremely unpleasant hissy fit.

- **Spontaneous conversations build a bridge of connection.** You want your teenager to know that you are there for her and love her no matter what. This bridge of connection keeps her protected. You want her to be able to come to you at any time. This is her safety net. You don't want her finding support and guidance solely from peers. She needs your input. I have talked to many girls who are afraid to talk with their parents because of how they may react. They want their parents' help, but don't want to feel ashamed or punished.

- **Spontaneous conversations make it easy for your daughter to come to you when she is in crisis.** If she can approach you with the smaller things, she can interrupt you when she really is in pain, like her first breakup. And if she is in real danger, like being stuck in a car with a drunk driver, she won't hesitate to ask you to pick her up.

- **Spontaneous conversations give your daughter a big gift.** You are giving the gift of your attention and care. You are listening to her! You are reflecting back to her that she matters and her stories matter. As a result, she feels you like her and that you enjoy her company, making her feel safe and secure in your presence.

- **Spontaneous conversations are good for *you*.** They help you with the "like" factor. Of course you love your daughter, but this allows you to like her and vice versa. This is a chance to see the relaxed side of your daughter. It keeps you current with her daily life—and it allows you to see your daughter in a new way!

How to Have a Spontaneous Conversation

Initiating spontaneous conversations can be frustrating for moms, because you can't force your daughter to have them on your own timetable. However there are certain things that you can do to help facilitate these conversations.

- Be open to interruptions; stop what you're doing and spend time with her when she initiates a conversation.

- Get curious about her world.

- Let her direct the conversation. Don't take the lead.

- Don't ask too many questions.

- Keep the conversation light. This is not the time to lecture. Keep it positive.

- Be responsive. Laugh if she is funny. Validate her feelings.

- Let her know you are on her side.

- Give her prompts that indicate you are listening, like "Wow" and "Really?"

- Relax and enjoy the interaction.

- Create Spontaneous conversations by getting your daughter out of the house. Take her to Starbucks after school, or go to her favorite lunch place.

Being Tuned In

It seems natural for a mother to be "tuned in" to her daughter. But in reality, healthy attunement can be challenging. You can err by being either hyper-tuned-in to *yourself* or by being hyper-tuned-in to *her*. Both are needed in the relationship but it's hard to find a balance. Let's take a closer look at both.

Your daughter tells you she's met some great guy at a football game. Her face is beaming, and she's jumping up and down. Where does your imagination go?

If you are triggered by fear, it's all over your face as it tightens up. Your expression is blank or angry. What comes out of your mouth will be antagonistic, like, "Who is this guy and how old is he?"

If, on the other hand, you are *not* triggered by fear, you're attuned to her feeling of excitement, and she sees that reflected in your face. What comes out of your mouth this time is, "Tell me about him."

Now let's say you're driving your daughter home from school and she tells you how stressful her day was. If you are thinking, "I bet it was, you didn't do any homework last night," and she feels your judgment, your daughter will clam up. If you have no preconceived ideas, then you are open to what she says. You respond with genuine care and concern, and she feels safe telling you that her best friend betrayed her.

Be careful not to project your own experience onto your daughter, as Andrea did with Natalie, or as Cathy, another of my mom clients, did with her daughter Jenny.

Cathy was very social in high school. She was involved in lots of activities and had lots of friends. Her daughter Jenny is an artist and has a few close friends. While Cathy was concerned about Jenny's social life, feeling she wasn't social enough, in reality her daughter was happy. But because her mom was always pushing her to join groups at school, Jenny felt she was a disappointment to her and avoided her whenever possible.

When you clearly see your daughter for who she is, rather than who you might want her to be, you can celebrate the differences. After Cathy worked with me, she saw that her daughter was content and happy. Mom started celebrating Jenny's creativity, and Jenny thrived with mom's approval.

When you are *hyper*-tuned-in to your daughter, there is an inevitable hyperreaction. If she sighs, you ask what's wrong. If she tells you she probably failed her history test, you freak out. If she sneezes, you want to take her to the doctor. When you are hyper-tuned-in, all you focus on is her. It's as if you don't exist. And if there are no boundaries between you and your daughter, you are going to be in danger of prying. Girls hate this, and your daughter will soon start hiding in her room.

You can't live your life through your daughter. It's not good for you, and it's not good for her. She needs you to be grounded and centered. If you are hyper-tuned-in to her 24/7, you will both be a mess. She needs her privacy and you need a life.

Being hyper-tuned-in to yourself is no better. When you are only tuned into yourself you only get one side of the story—yours. If you don't listen to your daughter you miss pertinent information and the context of her actions. Being hyper-tuned-in to yourself blocks you from having empathy toward your daughter. It also prevents authentic connection with your daughter, because you make it all about you. If she doesn't do well in school, she makes you feel like a failure. If she gets kicked off the team, you feel embarrassed around the other moms. If she comes home late, you're angry at her because she's inconvenienced your schedule. These may all be genuine feelings, but they will not bring any resolution to the issues. Your daughter is not motivated to change when it's solely about your feelings and she feels misunderstood.

Healthy attunement is a balancing act. You are tuned in to yourself as well as to your daughter. You bring the healthy, grounded parts of yourself into that attunement. Your actions and words line up. All the nonverbal signals (including tone of voice, eye contact, facial expressions, and gestures) are aligned with the vibe and feelings behind your words. This emotional communication allows you to feel your daughter's joy, which increases the positive feelings. This connection also allows you to feel your daughter's pain and yet remain grounded, which helps your daughter calm down. You are her rock. You soothe her distress with comfort and compassion. She feels safe in this nurturing connection.

How to Begin to Build a Positive Connection

So, how to achieve this perfect tuned-in-but-not-*too*-tuned-in state? Let's make this easy for you.

Start with Fun!

It's natural to ask, "Where do I start? My daughter and I are so far from what you're describing." I recommend you start by tuning into her positive emotions—and having fun!

Fun is not optional. It benefits you emotionally, builds a strong connection, decreases stress, and is good for your physiology. When you enjoy your life, your body creates more of the happy-body chemical, serotonin. When you are stressed, your body produces more cortisol, which decreases your happy-body chemicals.

Moms use the excuse that they are too busy to have fun. We put fun at the bottom of the priority list, because it feels extravagant. But it's really essential. You need the positive experiences with your daughter to buffer the hard times. The easiest way to connect is by sharing a positive experience. You want your daughter to remember the times you lay on the sofa watching a movie together or enjoyed a nice lunch with just the two of you.

Create positive associations with your daughter so she doesn't solely associate you with the wicked witch of the West. Positive associations help you with your "like" factor.

Many of you will say, "My daughter doesn't want anything to do with me." This is true for most of us: Most of our daughters will spend the majority of their time with friends. But they don't spend *all* their time with their friends. When you have a healthy relationship with your daughter, she can still spend time with you every day, even if it's only a half hour. The main reason your daughter avoids you is that she feels you're always on her back, telling her to do homework, clean her room, and come home by curfew. It's not healthy for your relationship to be Monitor Mom. Try having some fun with her.

Five Guidelines for Having Fun

It's so discouraging when you are trying to enjoy time with your daughter and it ends up in a big drama-fest. If you are clear ahead of time, you can avoid many of the common pitfalls by taking the following into consideration:

1. **It doesn't have to cost a lot of money.** There are many simple things you can do to create a positive experience. You can watch a DVD, have a nice lunch, get your nails done, and (of course) shop. If you are going to shop, decide how much money and time you're going to spend up front. If you don't, you're setting yourself up for a big drama-fest.

2. **You can agree on the activity beforehand.** What may be fun for you may not be fun for your daughter. You might want to go to the movies, but that would be too embarrassing for her because of the friend factor. Let her take the lead. Ask her what she would like to do. Give her some prompts like, "Where would you like to go to lunch?"

3. **Your agenda is to enjoy your time together.** This is a time to relax, not the time to bring up an issue, give advice, or pry.

4. **Make it a win.** Begin with something easy, such as taking her to lunch. Better to spend one hour having a positive experience than having an all-day stress-fest. You probably want to avoid bathing suit shopping.

5. **Be clear.** Tell your daughter you want to hang out with her and you have no hidden agenda. It might take some time before she believes you. You are establishing a new pattern.

Avoid Getting Hooked by Her Negative Emotions

Negative emotions are where it gets complicated for moms and daughters. It's incredibly hard to see your daughter brokenhearted and sinking into despair. It triggers all sorts of emotions, fears, and memories in us. But there is a healthy way to be attuned to your daughter without drowning in her feelings.

Healthy tuning-in involves:

- Being there

- Listening

- Validating your daughter's experience

- Showing her love and compassion

- Acknowledging feelings so she can move past them

Healthy tuning-in is not:

- Listening to her attack you

- Letting her disrespect or rage at you

- Validating distorted perceptions

- Being swallowed up by her fear, despair, and sadness

- Losing you in her story by obsessing about her life

So what do you do when your daughter's upset because her boyfriend just broke up with her? Here are a few ideas:

- **Be a calming presence.** Don't freak out and get emotional. You are her rock, so reassure her things will be okay. You are there to soothe her, just as when she was a baby in distress. You do that through empathy and compassion.

- **Don't dismiss your daughter's feelings.** Be careful not to write off her feelings by thinking, "She's about to start her period, and she's being too dramatic." Or, "She's making way too big a deal over this guy she's only gone out with once." You are evaluating her experience through adult eyes. Remember, this may be her first time to feel these feelings. When you dismiss them, she feels betrayed and misunderstood. This pours gasoline on the drama fire.

- **Don't give her a mother lecture.** I think the hardest part of dealing with your daughter's negative emotions is that you want to give her immediate feedback. She is in such despair and hopelessness. You know she is not seeing the big picture and is twisting information. You want to say, "Get a grip; it's not the end of the world." Don't.

- **Help her to calm down.** It's tempting to say "I told you he was a jerk," but this will just make her mad as a hornet. When this happens she is emotionally flooded with adrenaline, which causes her limbic system to be in control, and the cortex, the higher functioning part of the brain, goes offline—just as yours does when you are furious or panicked. She physiologically cannot take in any information until she calms down.

Later, when she is calm, you can have another conversation and offer advice.

When your daughter is upset, use the "calm-down" conversation. I have broken down the different components of this for teaching purposes. In reality, these components are organic; they flow and don't always happen sequentially:

- **Let her talk and you listen.** No matter how ridiculous or distorted the story is, just listen. If you are afraid she will talk all night long, set a timer for twenty minutes.

- **Don't interrupt her or give her any unsolicited advice.** She doesn't want advice right now; she wants you to understand and empathize.

- **Give her nonverbal cues that you are tuned in.** Make eye contact or nod. Don't text or answer the phone. (Your daughter needs the message that she is important much more than you need to see who is texting you.)

- **Be curious—but don't pry.** Being curious is an inside job. It's about your attitude. You put yourself in a mindset where you are curious about your daughter's heart, mind, and soul. This is a chance to get to know her world and how she perceives certain situations. Being curious is not invasive. You are following her story and clarifying it a little more. Ask, "What did the other girls think?" or "What did the teacher do then?" When you are curious, you are not up to anything except understanding her experience. Prying, on the other hand, is invasive. It starts from a judgmental place. You are going into monitor mode—"Were they drinking?" "When did your teacher assign the project?" "What kids were at the party?"— and she knows it. When your daughter thinks you're prying, she lashes out at you or retreats in her girl cave.

- **Reflect back her feelings.** Use comments like, "That sounds hard," "Wow, she sure did lose it," or "That was rude." This is difficult. You want to say, "Get a grip. Chill out. It's not a big deal." But this would invalidate her feelings. The paradox is, when you show empathy by reflecting her feelings, she can move past them.

- **Take her side.** I can hear you saying, "But she's dead wrong. There's no way I can take her side." I know this feels counter-intuitive, but the purpose of this conversation is to help her calm down. She calms down when she knows someone cares and is on her team. Try to see things from her perspective. She has just gotten home from a big soccer tournament and has to write a ten-page history paper and another big project is due the following day in English, and, to top it off, her best friend Jane said she was getting fat. Take her side by saying something like, "You do have a lot going on. It's overwhelming. I can't believe Jane said that." The next conversation with her, when she's less upset, you can talk about procrastinating.

Being Responsive

We have discussed how to be there for your daughter and how to be tuned in to her. The third way you create a secure attachment with your daughter is to be responsive. You want to make sure you're responding in healthy ways instead of reacting in ways that are detrimental to you and your daughter. Here are some dos and don'ts:

- *Do respond* **without reacting;** *don't react* **without responding.** Your daughter lost her phone. When you *respond and don't react,* you say, "I'm so sorry. When was the last time you remember seeing it? Where have you looked? Do you need my help?" If you *react and don't respond,* you say, "Seriously, we just bought you this phone. You are so irresponsible. Why do you lose everything? Do you know how much that phone costs?"

- *Do respond* **from a clear and calm place;** *don't react* **out of confusion, fear, or frustration.** Just as your daughter needs to calm down so that her higher brain is online, so do you. When you find yourself frustrated, give yourself the gift of a mom time-out. Take an hour for yourself: Take a walk, call a friend, get a pedicure. Drive to a local coffee shop and write in your journal. You need some time to detach from the drama to get clear.

- *Do respond* **with effective action;** *don't react* **by becoming hysterical and obsessing.** You discover your daughter is sexting. When you take effective action you sit down and talk to your daughter about her texts and pictures. You get counsel from a professional on what to do next. If you overreact, you may threaten, lecture, yell, cry, or shut down. You may not be able to sleep because you are so worried about her, but you don't take any effective action to deal with the sexting.

- *Do respond* **in a way that is consistent and reliable;** *don't react* **in inconsistent and unreliable ways.** Consistent and reliable interactions build trust between you and your daughter. She knows when she approaches you that you'll listen and care. This shows her that she is important to you. Because she knows how you are going to react, she is able to approach you when she is in trouble. Empty threats and promises build a wall of distrust between you and your daughter. She backs up because she's been disappointed. If she doesn't know how you are going to react, she will be guarded and start to avoid you.

I presume you get the message loud and clear: Be responsive, not reactive! This will stand you in good stead in just about any difficult circumstance that comes your way. Okay, now back to your teenager.

Many of you may be thinking, My daughter is independent and doesn't want my help. Yes, but you can still be responsive . . .

- **When she initiates everyday conversations.** Make time for spontaneous conversations and calm-down conversations. If she wants your attention, stop and give her your full presence for ten minutes. Be emotionally responsive. Laugh and smile.

Show that you are happy for her. Show her you care through a hug.

- **In times of transition.** Your daughter needs you even more in times of transition, whether it is to a different school, graduating from middle school, or moving to another city. The transition may be caused by a loss of a best friend, or a breakup with a boyfriend. During these times, she needs you to be her anchor, ready to respond. If she appears to regress during these times, know this is normal and will pass. Don't miss the opportunity to be close to her.

- **When your daughter shares her excitement.** Celebrate the big victories—and also the small ones. It's easy to miss the small victories. Any chance you can to celebrate her doing the right thing is hugely important. She feels your support and respect. Celebrate her getting a job, even if it's only stocking shelves at the local supermarket, or making a B on her paper.

- **When she needs your help.** Many girls don't know how to ask for help. This is where you need to respond to her needs even if she protests. If she is not making good choices and is in danger, you need to protect her. When she is stuck in a bad relationship or situation in school, you step in and help her get a strategy. Sometimes being responsive means hiring a tutor, therapist, or coach to get her on the right track.

* * *

Despite all the challenges, you can have a great relationship with your daughter when you have the right tools. When you don't "like" or enjoy your daughter, it's a red flag that something is off in the connection. Ask yourself if you are there for her, tuning in and responding in healthy ways. Enjoy her spontaneous conversations and stay grounded during the calm-down conversations. And above all, make time for fun. You can have good moments with your daughter every day when you are open and available.

CHAPTER 7

Why Your Daughter Is Hard-Wired for Drama and Why It's Not Personal

It was Sunday morning in Houston, Texas. Charlotte let her seventeen-year-old daughter, Chloe, sleep in while she went to church. When she came home, she found Chloe in the kitchen, standing on top of a chair, jumping up and down, and shrieking with excitement. "I just got a ticket to go with my friends to a private party with Lady Gaga in New York City tonight. I don't care what you say—I'm going."

Charlotte said she wouldn't pay for a plane ticket and went outside to give Chloe some space. When she walked back in, her daughter was on the computer looking up flights for New York and said, "I have enough money for a one-way ticket to New York City—and I'm going!" Charlotte took Chloe's computer and closed it. Outraged, Chloe yelled, "Then I'll buy a ticket at the airport. You're not going to ruin my life!" She then ran out of the house barefoot and took off in her car.

Charlotte panicked. She hoped her daughter wouldn't do anything stupid, but couldn't count on it. She got on the computer and transferred $500 from her daughter's account back into her own account, leaving only three dollars. Just then, she got a text from her daughter saying, "I bought a one-way ticket. Goodbye."

Charlotte knew her daughter was bluffing, but it still freaked her out. She texted Chloe and told her to come home *right now.* Fifteen minutes later, Chloe came home. Charlotte asked, "What were you thinking? You would have missed school. You had no money to fly home, catch a taxi, or buy food. Where were you planning on staying?"

I saw Charlotte in my office the following week. She was still reeling from that experience with Chloe. "What's wrong with her?" she asked me. "How could she make good grades in school, hold down a part-time job, and be this stupid? How could she do this to me?" I told Charlotte, "Chloe is not crazy or stupid," I told her. "But, like all teens, she is hard-wired for drama.

Teens are a quadruple threat for drama with their fluctuating hormones, undeveloped prefrontal cortex, dominant limbic system, and dopamine driver. So in a teenage brain, going to The Big Apple on a one-way ticket, with no money, sounds like an awesome idea. This is why Chloe needs you to step in and put the brakes on.

How do you make sense of your daughter's erratic behavior? It's easy to take things personally or feel like you are a total failure without the proper information. When you understand her brain development, it all starts to make sense.

Why Your Daughter Is a Quadruple Threat for Drama

Did your parents ever have a "What were you thinking?" moment with you when you were a teen? I think back at some of the things I did in high school and understand now that my teenage brain was under construction.

There are biological reasons why your daughter on occasion uses poor judgment, makes impulsive decisions, and has extreme mood swings. We can't blame it all on raging hormones, though they are definitely part of the equation. The biggest reason your daughter is innately dramatic is that major remodeling is going on in her brain. When you add hormone rushes to an immature prefrontal cortex, a very active limbic system, and a craving for the brain chemical dopamine, you are going to have drama. Knowing this will help you to not take things your daughter says and does personally, and can help you avoid getting pulled into the drama vortex. Understanding where your daughter is developmentally helps inform your parenting strategies. If you have ever wondered what was going on inside your daughter's brain, keep reading.

Fluctuating Hormones

Are your daughter's emotions like a roller coaster, with extreme highs and lows? Last night your daughter was in a great mood. You ate popcorn, laughed, and watched a movie together. This morning your daughter woke up, yelled at the dog, and slammed the bathroom door, yelling, "I hate my life. I'm a complete loser." Yes, there is a roller coaster and it's called hormones.

Hormones change significantly when your daughter enters puberty. This is the first time she experiences high levels of estrogen, and it's also the first time she experiences the monthly cycle of estrogen/progesterone surges. In her book, *The Female Brain*, Dr. Louann Brizendine states, "The first two weeks of the cycle, when estrogen is high, a girl is more likely to be socially interested and relaxed with others. In the last weeks of the cycle when progesterone is high and estrogen is lower, she is more likely to react with increased irritability and will want to be left alone." Dr. Brizendine goes on to say irritability can be extremely high at the end of the cycle because of maximum hormonal withdrawal.

Most moms are well aware of their daughter's menstrual cycles. You have experienced her meltdowns, temper tantrums, and anger outbursts one day, and the next day she is calm and in her right mind—after her period started. It's tempting to blame everything on hormones, but there's a lot more going on in her brain.

Undeveloped Prefrontal Cortex

My family loves to tell stories. One of our favorites is when my sister was thirteen and I was fifteen. My dad, sister, and I went to Memorial Park in Houston and hiked down to Buffalo Bayou. The bayou is brown, murky, and God knows what's in there. My sister saw that there was a rope swing connected to a big pine tree that swung over the bayou. She asked my dad if she could swing and jump into the water. Dad told her the water was full of sewage, disease, and poisonous snakes, and then said, "It's your decision, just use good judgment." My sister said "Thanks" and jumped into the water. My sister survived jumping into the disgusting water and we've kidded about it ever since. Today, my sister who has grown kids of her own would never jump into the sewage-filled bayou.

There is a reason for that. My sister's prefrontal cortex at age thirteen was undeveloped. In fact, the prefrontal cortex is not fully developed till age twenty-five. This is why, after you explain the logical consequences to your daughter, she still jumps into her teenage sewage hole. With a flaky prefrontal cortex, she makes impulsive "Woo hoo, this sounds like fun" decisions.

Behind the bone of your forehead is the prefrontal cortex, which is typically thought of as the CEO of the brain. It's the master control center that coordinates and integrates the whole brain and body together. Here are some examples of how a developed and undeveloped prefrontal cortex operates.

The prefrontal cortex is vital in adult life. It is responsible for:

Planning Ahead

- **Developed PFC:** You think through your week. You remember that you have a huge work deadline on Friday. You tell your friend you can't get together for dinner on Wednesday.

- **Undeveloped PFC:** Your daughter has three tests, a term paper, and a big history project due on Friday. It's Wednesday and she is very behind with her work. She begs you to let her go to a concert by her favorite band Thursday night.

Managing Emotions and Delaying Your Responses

- **Developed PFC:** You're driving to work and someone cuts in front of you. Thoughts of ramming their car go through your head, but you control yourself.

- **Undeveloped PFC:** Your daughter is driving to school and is running late. Someone cuts in the lane ahead of her. She lays down the horn, starts yelling obscenities, and gives him the finger.

Empathy

- **Developed PFC:** You're having lunch with a friend. She is a little quiet. You sense she's discouraged and you encourage her with compassionate words.

- **Undeveloped PFC:** You've had a long day. You walk in the door and tell your fourteen-year-old daughter Lourdes that you are exhausted and need help with dinner. Lourdes misinterprets the situation and answers, "Mom I always help you. Why are you mad at me?"

Self-Awareness

- **Developed PFC:** You come home from work and yell at your daughter because she's watching TV. You assumed she didn't do her homework, when she had already done it. Twenty minutes later you come in and apologize. You realized that you were tired and took out your frustration on her.

- **Undeveloped PFC:** You are trying to have a discussion with your daughter. You are calm and ask about her weekend plans. Jane, clearly reluctant to engage in the conversation, says, "I don't know, Mom." You ask another question and she explodes. "Mom, why are you so stressed out? *Stop!*" Actually, you weren't stressed out, she was.

Morality/Conscience

- **Developed PFC:** You get pulled over for a ticket and the policeman asks you if it's an emergency. You hesitate for a second and tell him no.

- **Undeveloped PFC:** Your daughter wants to go to the party with her friends. You ask your daughter if the parents are home. She lies and says yes. She does not feel bad for lying, but she will feel bad if she gets caught and grounded. Her morality and conscience are flaky at best during the teenage years, especially when it's fun and exciting.

Big Picture and Cause and Effect

- **Developed PFC:** You are working on your website, and you know it's going to be great when it's finished. You are putting in long hours and don't have much time for anything else. You know this is for a limited time and that the rewards are well worth it.

- **Undeveloped PFC:** Your daughter is in her junior year of high school, hates two of her classes, and is making a low C and a D. She refuses tutors because she would rather have fun with friends. She doesn't understand that this could keep her from getting into her dream college.

As you can see, an undeveloped PFC can significantly impact your daughter's choices and behaviors.

What makes this confusing for moms is that the PFC in a teenager is developing and is not fully developed at the same time. Think of the undeveloped PFC as flaky brakes that work some of the time. There are times your daughter uses good judgment and other times she throws caution to the wind. What you can expect is that her behavior is going to be unpredictable. With an undeveloped PFC, she is not going to plan ahead, manage her emotions, delay her responses, have empathy or insight, display steady morality, understand cause and effect, and see the big picture *consistently*. What this means is that your daughter needs you to be her brakes when her prefrontal cortex is offline. She needs your protection and guidance, contrary to what she may believe. She needs you to help her think through her actions and consider the consequences. You fill in the gap as her prefrontal cortex continues to develop.

An Active Limbic System

Because the limbic system is fully developed in the teenage years, it frequently takes charge over the undeveloped prefrontal cortex. This means that the emotional, reward-driven, impulsive, risk-taking limbic system is often running the show.

Deborah Yurgelun-Todd, a researcher at the McLean Hospital in Belmont, Massachusetts, discovered that the adolescent brain interprets emotional expressions differently than an adult's brain. Her most important experiment involved test subjects looking at a series of photographs of individual people. Each photograph showed a particular emotional state, including sadness, fear, surprise, and anger. The subjects were asked to identify the facial expressions. What they discovered surprised the researchers. Adults accurately identified the emotional states of the pictures, but the teens would often mistake sadness, fear, surprise, and even a neutral expression for anger. The study found that the adults relied on the prefrontal cortex to identify the facial expression while the teenagers relied on the amygdala in the limbic system. Teens rely on their gut reaction and frequently get it wrong. This explains why your daughter can say, "Mom, why are you so angry?" when you actually were just tired.

Teens misread facial expressions and misinterpret situations because they are not tapping into the wealth of information from the cortex. Without its input, their thinking becomes all or nothing, black and white.

This is why, when you say to your daughter, "You can't spend the evening with Rachel tonight. You have been gone the last four nights," she replies, "You never let me do anything. You hate my friends." To your daughter, it *feels* like she can't ever do anything. She has a gut reaction without reflecting on the fact that the last four evenings she was with her friends.

Another example of all-or-nothing thinking is your daughter telling you the first week of school that she loves her English teacher and he's the best teacher in the world. Six weeks later, she tells you that she hates him and he's a horrible teacher.

Addison is a fifteen-year-old girl who plays guitar and has a gorgeous singing voice. She told me that she was going to give up singing because she can't sing like Taylor Swift. Now that's all-or-nothing thinking!

This kind of thinking sets the teen up for discouragement, stress, anger, sadness, and hopelessness. This is so frustrating and heartbreaking for moms. It's incredibly hard to hear your daughter misinterpret situations that cause her unnecessary emotional pain. And it's easy for you to overreact to her overreaction. Your warning bells go off because of how desperate she feels. Now you're having your own stress response in your limbic system. (We talked about this in Chapter 2, and will look at it more closely in Chapter 8.)

The Dopamine Driver

Another reason your daughter is hard-wired for drama is because of dopamine, which is known as the "feel good" neurotransmitter. When the dopamine is flowing, she feels fully alive. During adolescence, there is an increase in the neural circuits utilizing dopamine that creates a drive for rewards. As a result, teens have a strong drive towards anything that would make them feel on top of the world, whether it's new exciting experiences, taking risks, or falling deeply in love.

The problem is that this drive is so strong that you can throw caution to the wind and downplay the facts or risks. Dr. Dan Siegel, in his book *Brainstorm*, describes this as *hyperrationality*. "This cognitive process comes from a brain calculation that places a lot of weight on the positive outcome and not much weight on the possible negative results," he writes.

You see this hyperrationality at play when Chloe was ready to buy a one-way ticket to New York to attend the Lady Gaga private party. The upside of flying to New York, seeing her friends, and going to this party was a ginormous dopamine jackpot. In light of the drive for the dopamine reward, she downplayed facts like *no money* and that her mom would have grounded her for the rest of the year.

The dopamine driver is at play when your daughter falls in love. Not only does the dopamine flow like Niagara Falls, but also she gets added perks from other "feel good" neurotransmitters, norepinephrine and serotonin. In his book *Love and Addiction,* Dr. Stanton Peele wrote that from the brain's point of view, falling in love is as powerful as a cocaine high. Yes, girls can act crazy when they are in love. They obsess, become fixated, and can be careless when chasing after the tall, handsome dopamine reward.

Teens are extremely vulnerable to alcohol, tobacco, and drug use because their brains are under construction. Because these substances release dopamine surges, they can be very addictive. The earlier teens are exposed to alcohol and drugs, the more likely they are to develop an addiction. Here's why.

During the teenage years, alcohol and drugs do more than kill brain cells, they interfere with neurotransmitters like dopamine. In his book *Why Do They Act That Way?*, Dr. David Walsh writes, "Whenever you chronically use a foreign substance like alcohol to trigger dopamine surges, the body stops producing the levels of dopamine that it normally needs." This creates a dependency on foreign substances like nicotine, alcohol, marijuana, or cocaine to feel good.

How the Teenage Brain Is Remodeled

If you have ever remodeled your home, you know it's a stressful time because you're getting rid of the old and replacing it with new appliances and furniture. In the middle of the new construction project, it can feel chaotic. You tolerate the stress of the remodeling because you know there will be a positive result. Each day you see a little more progress.

Your daughter's brain is also under major reconstruction, which is why she is a quadruple threat for drama. Fortunately your daughter won't be stuck in this remodeling phase forever, but her brain will continue to develop until she is twenty-five. Though this may feel like a long time, her judgment will improve, and she *will* become an adult. I promise.

This massive reconstruction project in the teenage brain is unlike anything that occurs at any other time in life, and is due to two very specific processes. One process is called myelination, which is similar to building new information superhighways throughout the brain. The other process is the blossoming and pruning of brain cell branches, which is like building new roads and shutting down old ones. This is done through the "use it or lose it" phenomenon, which is discussed below.

Building Superhighways: Myelination

Myelin is sometimes known as the white matter in the brain. It is the white fatty substance that covers the axon, the main cable of the neuron. This myelin sheath enables the passage of the electrical flow among interlinked neurons to flow up to 100 times faster. This new speed and coordination enables a more effective and efficient process. Think dirt roads with a few potholes (axons without the myelin covering) compared to a superhighway (axons with the myelin covering). Myelination is especially important because it links differentiated areas of the brain. For the teenage brain, this is especially seen between the lower cortical areas and the prefrontal cortex and the right and left hemispheres of the cortex. This is important because it allows your daughter to integrate her gut reactions of the lower brain with the higher brain processes like thinking things through, reflection and awareness, tapping into wisdom, weighing the risks, and seeing the big picture. In other words, myelination helps your daughter literally connect the *essential* dots.

Window of Opportunity: Use It or Lose It

There is a window of opportunity in the teenage years where, if you don't use it, you will lose it.

The teenage brain is undergoing its second phase of blossoming and pruning. The first phase happened around the time of the terrible twos. Blossoming is an intense growth spurt that overproduces the branches at the end of the brain cell. If you use these brain cells, the neural connections will stay. Experience is what causes these neurons to fire and wire together. If you don't use them, you will lose them and they will wither away. The neurons that get used repeatedly by experience are wired together into the brain's electrical networks.

When your daughter learns new dance choreography, plays a piano concerto, learns the periodic table, or learns how to speak French, she is using the opportunity and these neurons get stronger and stick around.

This blossoming of neurons offers amazing opportunities for your daughter. Learning how to play guitar or learning a new language will never be easier. You want to take advantage of this window of opportunity. If you don't use it, the brain assumes these neurons are expendable and they are pruned. This is why the teenage years are critical; if the brain is not used, it will not develop to its full potential.

Seven Ways You "Use It"

One of the joys in our lives is watching our children grow and blossom in their academic, creative, and physical abilities. We know it's important for them to be involved, challenged, and exposed to diverse interests and activities. Back when I was in high school, our parents kept us busy so we wouldn't get in trouble. Today, we know it's all about the teen's brain development. Teenagers love a challenge and so does the brain. The more the brain is exercised, the more it progresses, and whatever the brain does repeatedly is what the brain becomes good at.

Here are seven ways your daughter can develop her brain to its full potential:

1. **Pursue diverse activities.** Expose your daughter to a wide range of activities ranging from academics to creative pursuits to exercise. This could include travel, cooking, painting, singing, baseball, writing, riding a horse, playing an instrument, or attending a place of worship—and just about anything else she expresses even an iota of interest in.

2. **Develop perseverance.** It's important to learn the power of perseverance. You want your daughter to learn how to push and stretch herself, especially when it's hard. This is why your daughter benefits from a good coach who requires practice and rehearsals.

3. **Master a skill or talent.** Through perseverance, your daughter will learn to master a skill or talent. Nothing builds her self-esteem and confidence more than winning the race or learning a difficult piano concerto.

4. **Exercise creativity.** Creativity is the mother lode of brain development. It offers your daughter opportunities to develop her imagination through visual arts, writing a song, or expressing a character on stage. Creativity develops several facets at once. For example, if your daughter is a singer-songwriter, she develops her imagination and self-awareness. She builds her confidence and self-expression through performance, and learns the skill of playing guitar, and singing.

5. **Expand horizons.** Broaden your daughter's horizons by encouraging her to interact with different cultures and age groups. This helps her develop perspective and compassion, which breaks her out of a self-absorbed view of life. This won't happen if her world is solely limited to her group of friends.

6. **Express ideas.** Your daughter is realizing that she has her own thoughts and opinions. It is healthy for your daughter to express her ideas, even when they are different from yours. Debate teams at school are excellent places to develop logical thinking. You can also create a space to listen to your daughter's viewpoint and still maintain your authority.

7. **Communicate face-to-face.** Your daughter also develops her brain when she has face-to-face communication rather than texting or instant messaging. This includes connecting with people of all ages: family members, other adults, small children, and, of course, other teenagers. You want her to have

opportunities to practice active listening, to control her emotional impulses, and learn to think before speaking. Having
these repeated experiences in her teenage years strengthens
the wiring of her prefrontal cortex.

One more very important bit of neurophysiology to remember is
that your daughter's very busy teen brain needs a lot of sleep and
downtime to catch up with this hypergrowth season. It needs this time
to integrate all the new neural connections. When it looks like your
daughter is wasting time, she is actually doing something very important for her brain. She is allowing these new experiences to successfully wire into the brain's electrical system. The next time you see your
daughter being a couch potato, you can smile and know her brain is
actually being productive.

How You "Lose It"

If your daughter is not involved, challenged, connected, or engaged
in the real world, she is not "using it" and will "lose it." If she is under
too much pressure and stress from friends, parents, activities, and
school, she "loses it" because she defaults into the stress response of
fight, flight, or freeze, as you learned in Chapter 2.

Your daughter can also "lose it" with chronic use of drugs and alcohol, because it interferes with encoding new memories and with
short-term memory. That's why she can't remember what she said or
did after a night of binge drinking. Alcohol blocks a neurotransmitter
called glutamate, which enables neurons to store new memories and
to learn. Without the aid of glutamate, neurons that fire together *won't*
wire together. In his book *Why Do They Act That Way?*, Dr. David Walsh
writes, "Research shows that heavy alcohol use can impair adolescent
memory function by as much as 10 percent . . . . Thus adolescents who
drink a lot of alcohol end up having more memory and learning im-
pairment than adults who drink the same amount, because their
brains are more susceptible to damage."

Another way teen brains "lose it" is in the all-consuming digital
world.

The digital world has many benefits. The Internet is a great resource for learning, sharing information, connecting with people, and being entertained. But, oh, how things have changed since we were in high school. The new digital world catches us off guard because it's unfamiliar territory. When I was in high school, I had a phone with a telephone cord. I could only talk in the kitchen or in my parents' bedroom. There was some built-in accountability, but no more. With the ever-changing apps, instant messaging, texting, and skyping on cell phones, iPads, and laptops, monitoring your teen can feel like an uphill battle.

Shelly is a therapist and has a daughter who is in middle school. She came to my office extremely upset. She had just gotten her phone bill. Her daughter in seventh grade had sent 3,000 texts in the last month, and most of them were from midnight to 4:00 A.M. on school nights. Shelly was shocked, hurt, and felt extremely betrayed. She was unaware and unprepared. She didn't think about the addictive side of technology. She didn't consider her daughter's undeveloped prefrontal cortex and the dopamine thrill of connecting with boys at night. Once Shelly was educated about teens and cell phones, she realized it wasn't personal. Shelly intervened, put the brakes on, and took her daughter's cell phone at night.

There are three big reasons your daughter can "lose it" with electronics: too much screen time, inappropriate content, and chronic distraction.

In his book *Smart Parenting, Smarter Kids,* Dr. David Walsh writes, "Today the average school-aged kid spends more than fifty-three hours a week watching television, playing video games, or using the computer." Most teens don't get this much sleep in a week. A huge problem with this amount of screen time is that it is empty brain calories. These teens are not investing their attention, skills, and abilities in real life. This especially impacts their relationships.

Many a mom has complained that when her daughter has a friend spend the night, the daughter and her friend barely talk to each other. They can be in the same room texting other friends or even each other. As shocking as this is to us, in 2010 the Pew Internet & American Life Project found that face-to-face communication fell behind texting as a teen's favorite way of communicating with friends. This causes big problems for brain development. It's is a critical time for the teenage brain to wire networks for communication skills, empathic listening, and the ability to interpret and respond to nonverbal cues. And all of these skills take practice.

Your daughter can also "lose it" with inappropriate content. This past year, I saw a large number of teen girls in my private practice because they were caught sexting and had sent inappropriate pictures on line, only to find their private pictures had been forwarded to schools all over the community. We made mistakes when we were in high school, but these digital mistakes will always be remembered in the cyber world. Due to impulsivity, bullying, and the dopamine driver, these girls shared way too much, leaving them exposed to humiliation and shame.

A third way your daughter can "lose it" in the digital world is through chronic distraction. About a month ago, I was at Starbucks with a friend. At the table next to me were four teens working on a school project. They sat at a table with four laptops open, simultaneously texting and having conversations. I don't know how they could have accomplished anything.

Chronic distraction has become the new normal for this generation of teens. You see this when your daughter is doing her homework. She will argue with you that she can study while she is watching YouTube videos and texting her friends. She will tell you that she is better at multitasking than you are.

The truth is she cannot give quality attention to two things at once, especially when it's between instant messaging her friends and doing physics problems. Teens have learned to shift their attention rapidly from one thing to another, but they are still focusing on only one thing at a time. The problem is that when teens multitask, it becomes a chronic distraction and takes a toll on homework, relationships, and school performance. I'm sure you won't be surprised to learn that texting in the classroom decreases concentration and focus. It's important to eliminate and minimize the distractions of media. This is a crucial time for teens to develop focused uninterrupted attention in the prefrontal cortex.

* * *

How your teenage daughter responds and reacts to situations now is not how she will handle situations in her late twenties. This includes how she treats you. I can't tell you how many college girls have seen the light and apologized to their moms for how they treated them when they were in high school. Most of the drama, impulsivity, mood swings, anger, attitudes, and risk-taking behaviors are due to your daughter's brain still being under construction. It's not personal. You are not a terrible mom. Her imperfection is normal. You need to let this sink in, because if you take this personally, you're going to turn into a Drama Mama.

CHAPTER 8

How Good Moms Become Drama Mamas

You may have a drama queen daughter, but as a mom, you can easily get pulled into the drama vortex and become a Drama Mama. That's what happened to Karen and her daughter, Ellen.

Karen is a professional who works for a nonprofit organization. Her husband, Lee, is a high school English teacher. Mom came to the first session with Ellen when her daughter was a junior in high school.

I met with Ellen alone for the first thirty minutes. I learned that she played lacrosse and generally made good grades. I also learned that she babysat in her neighborhood and worked twennty hours a week in a clothing store.

When I asked Ellen why her mom wanted her to come to therapy, she said, "My mom says I'm lazy and a disappointment. She also says I'm throwing my life away and I'll be lucky to get into college." Ellen was completely detached as she spoke.

At this point, I invited Mom into the room. Immediately, Ellen's face flushed. She looked down and tensed up.

I asked Karen how I could help, and in front of her daughter she said, "Ellen is violent and infantile." She described a situation in which she had walked past Ellen's bedroom, expecting to see her studying for a test, and instead found her laughing and talking on the phone. "When I told Ellen to do her homework she threw her phone across the room. Then she stormed out of the house, knocking chairs over and slamming the front door."

Ellen was glaring at her mother. Her mother's words angered her, and she responded, "You're full of it. You call me stupid and lazy, when I'm making A's and B's in my accelerated classes. Then you tell me I'll never get into any college because I'm unfocused and unmotivated. That was the day I stopped trying to please you."

When I spent time alone with Mom, I found out why she was hyperfocused on Ellen's grades. Karen told me that she hadn't gone to a "good" college and believed this was the root of all her problems, causing her to settle for an unfulfilling career and disappointing marriage. She resented her life, was very unhappy, and was terrified that Ellen would repeat her mistakes (does this last phrase remind you of any earlier moms?).

Desperate, Karen fired off her big guns—labeling, shaming, threatening, yelling, and predicting doom to try to get her daughter to change her ways. The problem was that these tactics destroyed their connection and ticked Ellen off while eroding her motivation and self-esteem. Shame never brings out anyone's best; it catapults "the shamer" and "the shamed" into the limbic dance of fight, flight, or freeze.

To turn this around, Karen needed to identify her superloaded trigger, which was seeing her daughter making one of *her* high school mistakes—or thinking that's what she was seeing. She also needed to understand her part in escalating the drama, and learn constructive new ways to respond to her daughter.

This chapter isn't about blaming moms; it's about empowering them. A Drama Mama is not empowered. She has lost control of her emotions, words, and actions. When you lose control, you also lose credibility, effectiveness, and, ultimately, a positive connection with your daughter. Though we don't like to talk about it, many good moms often morph into Drama Mamas with their teenage daughters. Here's why.

How You Are Set Up to Become a Drama Mama

By now you're starting to see the drama setup. When you believe the Powerless Parenting Messages, lack clarity, and lose your "I feel good" energy, and you combine this with a teenage daughter who is hard-wired for drama (they *all* are, by the way, not just yours), you're in danger of becoming a Drama Mama.

Contrast Your Life with Your Daughter's Life

There's a big contrast between where you are in your life and where your daughter is in hers. Aside from the stress of raising a teenager, you may feel stuck in a routine, a relationship that isn't working, or a job you don't like. You're saddled with responsibilities and commitments while your daughter is most likely having fun. Let's look at the contrast:

- Your daughter's only responsibility is school and a few chores; you are loaded with financial obligations as well as work, home, and family responsibilities.

- She has time to chill out in her room; you don't have a minute to sit down.

- She goes to Europe during spring break; your big trip is to visit your aging parents.

- You spend money on clothing, makeup, a smartphone, and a laptop for your daughter; you don't buy anything for yourself because you're saving money for her college education.

- She enjoys a new relationship and romance; you are sick and tired of your partner.

- You worry she is having sex; you haven't had sex in the longest time.

- She is learning new skills and being challenged; you are stuck in a rut.

- She is hanging out with her friends every day; you'd be happy to see your best friend once a month.

- Her future is wide open and exciting; yours seems bleak because you no longer know what you want and feel that it's too late to make changes.

- Her body is young and toned without even trying; yours takes a lot of work.

- She feels entitled and wants more; you feel devalued and expect less.

Resentment can easily creep in if you are unsatisfied with your life and see your daughter having a grand time. All it takes is one Drama Button pushed and you're in full-fledged Drama Mama mode.

Beware of the Drama Buttons

A Drama Button is on a hair trigger. It can go off with little pressure. It generates fears, issues, and memories. A Drama Button can be universal or personal to you; in either case, it takes you straight to the reactive part of your lower brain. This is an automatic and quick reaction that triggers your stress response of fight, flight, or freeze. When your buttons are pushed, you go from zero (calm) to a hundred (Drama Mama) in a split second. Here are some Drama Buttons to watch for.

The Disrespect Button Your Disrespect Button gets pushed when your daughter fires off hostile, rude, dismissive, and mean-spirited comments. It can make you feel like her punching bag. She belittles, dismisses, and challenges your authority and power. One mom describes it this way: "The Disrespect Button goes off with the sassing eye rolls, and when my daughter walks away when I'm trying to explain something, all she says is, 'Whatever.'"

The Guilt Button When your daughter pushes your Guilt Button, it's because she isn't getting what she wants. She starts with a remark like,

"Mom, if you love me you'd buy me the newest iPhone." Comments like this throw you into an inner conflict. If you give in, your daughter is happy, but you feel like a bad mom. If you say no, she gets angry and you still feel like a bad mom. You feel misunderstood because she twists your motives to get what she wants. Your Guilt Button is pushed when you get comments like: "Mom, you know if you don't let me go to this concert with Sophia she won't come to my party next month, and if she doesn't come, neither will any of the other popular kids. Do you want me to spend my birthday with losers?"

The Taken-for-Granted Button   Your Taken-for-Granted button is pushed when you are made to feel unappreciated. You bend over backwards for your daughter and expect, in return, that she will be grateful and do what you ask. Your button gets pushed when she breaks promises, lies, exhibits a defiant attitude, and does not keep her end of the bargain. One mom said, "After volunteering at a band competition all day, I ask her to do one simple thing—load the dishwasher. She started screaming at me, and, well . . . that pushed my buttons." Another mom said, "What gets me is that everything is expected. After being her chauffeur, maid, and social coordinator, she doesn't even say thank you. My button got pushed when I told her to be grateful, and she said, 'That's your job.'"

The Fear Button   The Fear Button is the hottest button of all. When it's pushed, it brings up issues from the past like, "I don't want you turning out like my ex-husband" or "Don't make the same mistakes I made." There are also the here-and-now Fear Buttons like "She's taking drugs" or "She's going to get pregnant." This leads to you to think, "What if I can't fix this? If she's not okay now, what will she be like in the future?" Fear Buttons trigger explosive reactions because they are about your daughter's well-being and safety.

The problem with Drama Buttons is that once they've been pushed, you're offline from your higher brain and missing important information. This puts you in stress response, with all-or-nothing thinking. You can't see the big picture and jump to conclusions rather than reading the situation accurately. And when you react, you trigger a reaction from your daughter. Now both of you are doing the Drama Dance. (Yes, we called it "the limbic dance" in Chapter 2, but I think this has a nice flare. And it's good to practice your flexibility—it will help you through the next few years!)

How to Recognize a Drama Dance . . . and Avoid It

To understand the Drama Dance, you need to understand family systems. A family is composed of individual members, but also its own little emotional universe made up of interactional patterns among family members. One person's behavior doesn't occur in isolation; it impacts everyone in the system. When one member gets emotionally charged, the reaction time between family members is lightning fast. When these automatic reactions repeatedly occur over time, they turn into predictable patterns. They turn into the Drama Dance.

I wish I could tell you that it's all your daughter's fault, but it isn't; you are part of the family system too. I'm not saying it's all your fault either. Your daughter's actions, feelings, and words interact with yours. I know this first hand. When my daughter was twelve, I often was hooked in her Drama Dance and would justify my reactions to myself: "Okay, yes I'm yelling and pounding my fist on the table, but she's not going to treat me or anybody else this way. I need to put her in her place." (Being peri-menopausal didn't help.) What really happened was that my daughter lost control—and so did I. She got angry and said things she shouldn't—and so did I.

No mom feels good after she participates in the Drama Dance; I know I never did. But it doesn't help you or your daughter to beat yourself up about it. Actually, when you extend grace to yourself for losing control, it allows you to extend that same grace to your daughter. Being compassionate with yourself allows you to be compassionate with others. More important, it allows you to reflect on your actions and reactions.

The easiest way to dial down the drama is to take 100 percent responsibility for your part in the dance. Believe me, there is something deep in moms that wants to blame it all on their daughters. It takes honesty, courage, and compassion to examine how your words and actions escalate the situation. You may have good motives, but still stoke the fire. Nothing good comes from the Drama Dance. It is destructive to you and your daughter, and the consequences get worse over time. The good news is that the dance will change when just one person changes her part in it. It's not going to be your daughter; she's hard-wired for drama. It's up to you to take the lead; you're the one with the fully developed brain.

Let's look at five types of Drama Dances moms typically fall into.

The Argue Dance Arguing is not a conversation; it is a limbic dance. (In fact, all five Drama Dances are.) You may start off thinking you are setting a limit with your daughter with statements such as, "You can't go out this weekend; you need to bring up your grades." Your daughter then starts arguing because she's not interested in what you have to say or open to logical explanations. She will hook you with a statement like "Mom, you just want me to be perfect," which is both illogical and tangential. If you take the bait and argue that "I don't want you to be perfect, but you need to pull up your grades," she'll escalate it with more passion and emotion: "You think I'm stupid. Everything I do is wrong." What will keep you hooked in the Argue Dance is the mistaken belief that if your daughter sees it from your point of view and understands your reasons, she will back down and agree. Oh, sweet reason! If only it worked that way. This won't happen because all she really cares about is seeing her friends. If the argument continues, it will escalate from grades to character bashing to spinning out of control with raised voices and storming off and slamming doors.

The Battle Dance If the Argue Dance gets hot enough, it turns into the Battle Dance. The stakes are higher here. It's bigger than winning an argument; it's about winning the war. You pull out the big weapons—shaming, labeling, belittling, mocking, or even slapping;

things you would never say or do normally seem necessary in the heat of the battle. Moms justify their actions by thinking, My daughter started it. I'm just defending myself. I'll show her how it feels. She won't listen to me any other way. (I had one mom tell me that she has to slap her daughter in the face to get her to stop being disrespectful. You can imagine how successful that is! It may shut her daughter up, but it sure doesn't make her respect her mother.) All these big-gun behaviors may feel justified, but the bottom line is that you are doing grave harm.

Negative labels are hard to shake. Labeling your daughter selfish, lazy, stupid, mean, rude, or obnoxious, or calling her a slob, a slut, a liar, or a loser attacks her core essence and damages her self-esteem. A label is a proclamation that says, "Who you are and who you will be is flawed and unlovable." And do you remember Janice and Wendy from Chapter 3? It's worth repeating Brené Brown here: "If a child *tells a lie,* she can change that behavior. If she *is a liar*—where's the potential for change in that?" I cannot stress enough how harmful labels can be.

You can belittle your daughter in other ways as well. You can belittle by constantly pointing out her faults, or by rubbing her nose in past failures, or by making negative comments like, "Good luck finding any man who would put up with you."

The worst kind of belittling is mocking, and, yes, I know your daughter may have started it, but that doesn't make it right. Mocking is disrespect at the root. It acts out contempt and disdain. It comes across in a sarcastic and ridiculing manner like, "Oh, that's right, you're a great driver. That's why you've had two tickets and a fender bender in the last month."

Moms get hooked in the Battle Dance because they think they can win the battle by force. This translates into defeating the enemy (your daughter) and making her the loser. The belief is that if you tell her the stark truth and shock her enough, she will want to change her ways. All she takes from this is that once again, you are degrading her. No impetus to change there.

Your daughter may have a tough exterior but shaming tactics will only damage her psyche. It won't motivate her to change or get any helpful message. Because of where she is developmentally, she'll hear, "My mom's given up on me and hates me." These tactics will greatly damage your relationship and erode her confidence.

The Threatening Dance   At the core of the Threatening Dance is fear. Because you are scared or even panicked, you try to *scare* your daughter into changing by making negative predictions about the future or threatening her in the present.

Examples of negative predictions are . . .

- "If you keep dressing like a slob, you'll never get a boyfriend."

- "If you keep eating like that you're going to be huge."

- "If you don't improve your grades, you'll be lucky to get a job at McDonalds."

A threat feels like a consequence, but it's not. A threat is impulsive, punishing, and is not realistic. Some threats *appear* real, like, "If you bring home any D's, you are grounded for the rest of the year," but your teen knows that you won't go through with it, and the threat is, therefore, unrealistic.

Other examples of unrealistic threats are . . .

- "If you keep acting like this I'll send you to your father's."

- "If you come home drunk, I'll never let you drive the car."

- "If you sneak out of the house, I'll call the police and have you arrested."

What keeps moms hooked in this dance is the belief that they can control their daughters through threats, and that if it's not working it's only because the threats aren't big enough. Threats will never work. Fear begets fear. Back in the stress response of fight, flight, freeze, there is no happy ending. Your daughter can threaten back, "Fine, then I'll leave," which escalates your fear and causes you to threaten an even more dire consequence. Because most of these are empty threats, you lose credibility.

The Avoidance Dance The Avoidance Dance may not feel like a dance to you, but it is. It happens when you are done with your daughter. When you are immensely frustrated, spent, worried, disappointed, or wounded, you just don't want to deal with her anymore. The emotionality is so intense that you react by distancing yourself from her. You stop making an effort to communicate. You may avoid her by spending more time at work or in volunteer activities. Sometimes you may purposely ignore her when she walks past you in the room, or refuse to engage when she tries to share something with you. You are withholding connection to protect yourself or to punish her.

The Avoidance Dance also happens when you try to dodge and ignore all conflict. One mom told me this story about her best friend. Paloma came home from work early. She walked into the house and she heard noises from the second floor. When she leaned in and listened, she realized that her sixteen-year-old daughter and her boyfriend were having sex in *her* bedroom. *You* might have stormed into the bedroom and thrown that boy out of bed, but not Paloma.

She was horrified. This went against her values. She felt betrayed; she froze up, and didn't know what to do. She left the house, got back into her car, and drove around the block. She then drove back up the driveway and made lots of noise when she walked into the house. She wanted to make sure her daughter and her daughter's boyfriend heard her. They did, and ran out the back door. Now that's avoidance! A few minutes later, her daughter came home and both Paloma and her daughter pretended nothing had happened. Here's the crazy thing. Paloma never talked to her daughter about the incident. Mom avoided conflict with her daughter, but she felt she had betrayed her own deep-rooted religious values by pretending the sexual behavior was not taking place.

Moms get hooked in the Avoidance Dance in order to evade all conflict or bad feelings. The truth is the Avoidance Dance amplifies both external and inner conflict. Because you fear your daughter's reaction, you avoid confronting her. This gives your daughter too much power, and leaves you feeling disempowered as a parent. Boundaries, consequences, and guidelines are not enforced, and your daughter is on her own, with no accountability, and left unprotected. If your daughter can't get a positive response and guidance from you, she may escalate the situation until she finally gets your attention—and it surely won't be positive. Ignoring your daughter's warning signs will most certainly land you in a crisis.

The Nice Dance The Nice Dance has similarities to the Avoidance Dance. They both dodge conflict. Being nice is a great quality. But sometimes being nice is another form of the "disease to please." You want to please or be nice to your daughter, and will do so at your expense (and, really, her expense). Because your daughter is hard-wired for drama, "nice" doesn't always work. Her behavior needs to be dealt with by setting limits and boundaries and having honest conversations. In the Nice Dance you don't deal with her negativity. You silence that part of you that ought to hold her accountable for her actions. Instead, you maintain the façade of being nice. You can't keep this up, though. The nicer you are, the more she will take advantage of you. At some point, you will explode or implode.

Moms embrace the Nice Dance because that's what they have been taught to do. You think that if you keep being nice to your daughter, she will be nice to you. Because her brain is under construction, she needs other help from you besides being nice. She needs you to be strong, assertive, and courageous. It takes qualities like these to put the brakes on and protect her.

How You Can Create a New Dance

The Drama Dance, fueled by out-of-control feelings and misguided instincts, takes you and your daughter on a downward cycle. You do more of the very thing that amplifies the drama, be it more arguing, battling, threatening, avoiding, or even being nice. It's time to create a new dance. You do this by, first, dialing down *your* drama and regaining your perspective and clarity again. Once you feel empowered, you are ready to lead the Empowered Dance.

Dial Down *Your* Drama

To dial down your drama, you turn down the intensity of your feelings. You start by physically removing yourself from the dance in order to calm down. This may feel counterintuitive and almost impossible when you're in the heat of it. You may feel that if you walk away, you are letting your daughter win, but in fact, walking away is the first step to the Empowered Dance. You have to be intentional about calming down; it will not happen naturally. What helps you to calm down and turn the situation around is learning how to lay all the frustration and feelings aside.

Calm Down It's of utmost importance to calm down. Remember, when you are emotionally flooded you are offline from your higher brain. Calming down automatically gets you back online. But because calming down is challenging, you need a strategy:

- **Take a break.** If you and your daughter are getting emotionally flooded, stop the Drama Dance immediately by saying, "We need to take a break, I need to calm down, and we can talk about this later." If you say, "*You* need to calm down," she'll shout, "I *am* calm, dammit!" Give yourself permission to take a break. Tell yourself, "I can't see a way through this, but I will when I can calm down."

- **Contain the situation.** You can't solve the problem when the situation is hot, but you can contain it. This means postponing a decision, taking her keys for the night, or having her stay home. Try communicating to her through texting. This helps de-escalate the drama and gets your point across.

- **Detach by distracting.** Do something that will distract you from the drama. This is a quick way to calm down. And while you're at it, choose something that will replenish your good energy. Take a walk with your dog or go to the gym, watch a TV show or play a game on your computer, or buy your friend a birthday card and present.

Lay It Down   After you have calmed down, you need to "lay it down." Lay down everything that was stirred up in the Drama Dance. The dance can be physically finished, but you can still be replaying it in your head 24/7. Your brain gets stuck like a broken record. Every time you relive the situation in your mind you suffer, get mad, or panic again. It's not helping you at all. This isn't new information, and it doesn't solve the problem. You can lay it down by doing the following:

- **Give it over.** Sometimes the fear, disappointment, and anger are too much for you. This is where you can put your daughter's concerns in the hands of a Higher Power. You can do this through verbal or written prayer. You can use visualization, where you see your daughter whole, calm, and full of light. This is not about passivity. It's about getting free of the burden and the struggle.

- **Remember the positive.** You lay down the struggle to remember the positive. It's not all bad. You remember the big picture. Your daughter has strengths and positive attributes. You remember the times when she has listened to you and made good decisions. You remember how you worked though the last issue and came out stronger. You remember what classes she's passing, that you had a good day together yesterday, that her teachers and friends love her, and that she has earned an A in social life.

- **Practice mindfulness.** Mindfulness is a mental activity where you bring all your attention and awareness to the present moment. This allows you to experience the here and now. It allows you to observe your feelings, struggles, and frustrations from a distance. Instead of being in anger, you are observing your thoughts *about* anger. This gives you some space to analyze your struggle and see it from a different perspective. When you are relaxed, being present happens naturally. But when you are dealing with difficult emotions it's easy to get preoccupied—and this is where mindfulness exercises can be very helpful. If you are new to mindfulness you may want to read *Mindfulness for Beginners: Reclaiming the Present Moment—and Your Life* by Jon Kabat-Zinn. The exercises in this book will help you calm down your turbulent emotions and will enable you to observe your inner processes without judgment and with compassion. You can also try a yoga class; many moms feel this has literally saved their sanity, if not their life.

Turn It Around Once you have quieted your mind, you are back online and ready to turn it around. Let's revisit the Drama Dance with a new set of lenses. Ask yourself these questions:

- Which of my Drama Buttons got pushed?

- What tactics did my daughter use and how did I react?

- How do I justify my reaction?

- Which Drama Dance did I participate in?

- What kept me hooked?

- What memories did it bring up?

Your awareness moves you forward. When you can identify your part in the drama, you can change the dance. Learn from your past experience to avoid future pitfalls. Think of your front yard as a minefield, where the mines are covered with grass. If you don't know where the mines (the Drama Buttons) are hidden, they are bound to blow up when you walk through the front yard. If you identify them, they can be marked and you can dodge them the next time you leave your house.

Do the Empowered Dance

The Empowered Dance starts with an Empowered Mom. In systems theory, it only takes one to change the dance. In the Empowered Dance, you take the lead. It takes two to do the Drama Dance. You are not dependent on your daughter's dance. If you don't react when your daughter presses your Drama Buttons, if you don't respond to her tactics and escalate, there is no Drama Dance. The Empowered Dance does take practice. You may slip back into some old drama moves, but step back, evaluate it, and turn it around.

Become the Empowered Mom   The Empowered Mom learns from the past. She knows it's easy to react to her teenage daughter, go offline from her higher brain, and find herself in stress response. She knows that if she is not intentional, she will turn into Drama Mama. She knows that to be the Empowered Mom, she needs to focus on the many facets that have been addressed in this book.

This is why the Empowered Mom . . .

- Takes care of herself.

- Dismantles the F-bomb.

- Knows perfection is not the goal and is gentle with herself.

- Has clarity for herself—and is crystal clear with her daughter.

- Replenishes her good energy.

- Maintains a good connection with her daughter.

- Remembers that her daughter's drama is not personal and that the teenage brain is under construction.

Learn New Dance Steps   The Empowered Dance begins with your decision. It is proactive and intentional. It keeps the big picture in mind and doesn't focus on the drama. It is strategic and purposeful, leaving you and your daughter empowered.

There are four steps for the Empowered Dance:

1. **Decide beforehand.** Decide today that, no matter what, you won't participate in the Drama Dance. Decide that you will take the lead in the Empowered Dance. Know beforehand *who* you want to be and *how* you will interact with your daughter, even in full-fledged drama episodes.

You do this by creating an intention like, "I intend to be strong, loving, patient, centered, and wise in challenging situations" or "Despite the difficult times, I intend to enjoy my daughter and remember her strengths, giftedness, and resiliencies."

In the Empowered Dance, you are the model. You show your daughter how to have self-control, respect, and strength in disagreements. You model to your daughter how you want her to act and how you want to be treated. You also do this by taking ownership of your own drama and inviting her into the empowered Dance: "Jill, I don't want to fight with you all the time. I want our home relaxed, where your friends will be comfortable. I'm sorry for losing my temper with you and saying things that hurt you. It's my responsibility to calm down."

2. **Stay connected.** The Empowered Dance is happening all the time because it's all about maintaining connection. You intentionally build positive interactions with your daughter every day. This builds up a surplus of positive experiences that get you through the hard times.

3. **Anticipate and prepare.** The Empowered Dance is proactive. You anticipate when your daughter will be edgy and stressed, like during finals or a break-up with her boyfriend. You see the signs when your daughter has turned into Limbic Girl. Your awareness helps you become internally prepared. You can put up your metaphorical mother shield and not let her drama darts into your heart. Anticipation and preparation enable you to be grounded and stay online.

4. **Wait for strategic moments.** In the Empowered Dance, timing is everything. You know that if either of you is emotionally flooded, it's not the time to work through problems. You wait for strategic moments when both of you are calm to bring up and process the red-hot issues.

Your goal is not to punish, belittle, or put your daughter in her place; it's to empower her. Your goal is to empower her to exercise self-control, make good decisions, evaluate past mistakes, and motivate her to move forward. You implement this through the Potent Parenting Tools that I discuss in the next chapter.

* * *

There are many reasons good moms become Drama Mamas. However, when you are equipped with the right information and awareness, you can say goodbye to her. Your awareness moves your forward. By identifying Drama Buttons and Drama Dances, you can learn to avoid the triggers with your daughter. The Empowered Mom creates a new dance by taking the lead and intentionally moving forward with her daughter in the Empowered Dance.

CHAPTER 9

How to Discipline Your Teenage Daughter

It was ten o'clock on what had been a long Friday. Deborah told her twelve-year-old daughter, Rebecca, to clean her room and go to bed. She was done being the "mom" and ready to relax. After taking a hot bath, Deborah picked up her current book and got into bed.

Five minutes later, Rebecca started slamming doors. She didn't want to go to bed and the last thing she wanted to do was clean her room. When Deborah called, "Go to bed *now!*" her daughter stormed into her mom's room and started complaining, "You never spend time with me. You don't care about me. All you care about is a clean house." Deborah's efforts to calm her down failed as Rebecca cranked up the drama. This went on for nearly an hour, until she threw Deborah's antique vase at the mirror, shattering both. At this point, pushed to the edge, Deborah lost it completely. She shouted louder and louder until Rebecca collapsed in tears and Deborah literally dragged her, kicking and screaming, back to her room.

The following week Deborah came to my office. After hearing her story, I asked about Rebecca's consequence. She just stared at me until, after a minute of silence, she said, "Oops, I forgot to give Rebecca a consequence."

Here's the deal: Yelling at your daughter feels like a consequence, but it isn't. In fact, Deborah admitted that later in the weekend she agreed to let Rebecca have a friend spend the night . . . and gave them money to go shopping the next day.

What did Rebecca learn from all of this? She learned that if she throws a big enough fit, she doesn't have to clean her room, she can have a friend spend the night, and she can go shopping with money her mother gives her. In other words, Deborah inadvertently rewarded Rebecca for her bad behavior.

I helped Deborah see that punishing Rebecca by yelling and dragging her off to bed didn't instruct or change her daughter's behavior in a positive way; it only escalated the drama. "Then what's the best way to discipline my teenage daughter?" she asked.

This is a question I hear from moms all the time. First, we need to understand the foundation of empowered discipline.

The Foundation of Empowered Discipline

You need a solid foundation before using the potent parenting tools that you'll find later in this chapter. "Empowered discipline" is about being clear and having the right mindset. Without this, it's easy to lose your perspective. When your daughter gets into trouble or defies you, it can feel like the end of the world. Intense feelings like panic, anxiety, anger, and hopelessness can strike at lightning speed. This brings confusion and chaos into your home, straining family relationships. The foundation is there to keep you grounded. It reminds you that you are *for* your daughter, that all teenagers make mistakes. It keeps you clear about the rules, boundaries, consequences, and what your daughter really needs.

The Point of Discipline

For many, the word *discipline* has negative connotations but, according to the Online Etymological Dictionary, this word comes from the Latin word *disciplina*, which means "instruction given, teaching, learning, knowledge." Discipline does not have to be seen as negative; it's about giving your daughter what she needs to move towards adulthood. Empowered discipline is about equipping, guiding, teaching, motivating, and ultimately, *empowering your teen.* It is not about putting your daughter in her place, getting your anger out, or showing her how she made you suffer.

Recently, Susan and her eighth-grade daughter, Janna, came to my office. They were there because Janna had been cutting her wrist. "When my mom saw the cuts, she grabbed my wrist and started yelling at me," Janna said. "I completely freaked out," Susan then admitted with embarrassment. "I took a razor blade and cut my wrist in front of Janna so she could see how she made me feel." Obviously, this was not helpful in any way.

The question to ask when using discipline is not, "How could she do this to me?" it's, "What does my daughter need to learn?" Remember that your daughter's brain is under major reconstruction and she is a quadruple threat for drama. She needs you to put on the brakes. She needs your guidance and protection. She needs you to be an example.

Effective discipline is intentional, not reactive. You must choose to take a positive approach and to adopt a positive mindset—because this will not happen naturally. When you have to deal with your daughter's boyfriend drama, failing grades, broken curfews, full-blown disrespect, temper tantrums, or excessive partying, it pushes you to the edge and your gut reaction is going to be anything but positive. Yet, with the right perspective, it's possible to discipline (teach) your daughter effectively.

How to Think About Your Daughter's Mistakes

An important part of your mindset will depend on how you think about your daughter's mistakes. Whether you are able to see her missteps as a normal part of her development will determine how you respond to her. You must accept that she is going to have slip-ups, which is not the same thing as condoning or ignoring them. You know she still needs your input and guidance—and your discipline. After all, this is why she is still living under your roof. While you're not happy about her mistakes, you mustn't be rattled or horrified by them either. As your daughter walks from adolescence to adulthood, you must have realistic expectations. Just like a toddler learning to walk, when she falls you should not be surprised. Instead of focusing on the falls, however, your attention should be on helping her get back on her feet. You need to help steady her until she can walk through adulthood on her own.

If you believe that mistakes are *not* a normal part of a teen's development, this will take you down a very different road. You will be headed for harsh judgment and shame, either directed towards yourself or towards others. Perhaps you will judge someone else's daughter harshly for getting into trouble, and may even feel better about yourself as a parent as a result—until your daughter makes her own mistakes. Then, real or imagined, you may feel judged by other parents or family members. You may feel they are talking behind your back, saying things like, "She must not be a very good mom if her daughter was caught smoking weed," or "Where was her mom when her daughter sent inappropriate pictures to boys?"

When you feel judged by others, it changes how you see your daughter, and how you feel about her. It's easy to turn on your daughter by being judgmental. Instead of appreciating her, you feel disdain. Instead of seeing her gifts and abilities, you may see her as flawed, inferior, dirty, or unworthy. The most tragic part of your daughter's mistakes is that you lose respect for her, and she will pick up on this. If she continues to feel this judgment, she will internalize your feelings and believe she is flawed and unworthy.

You are not a bad parent if your daughter makes mistakes, even big ones. The belief that "If you were doing a good job as a mom, your daughter would be well behaved" just isn't true. It's not about *making* your daughter behave. A good parent slowly lets out the leash of freedom and responsibility while the teen is still at home. You want your daughter to learn how to exercise self-control and implement good decisions. Part of the risk of letting out the leash is that she can make bad decisions. And some of those bad decisions can have long-term ramifications, no doubt: a pregnancy, drug addiction, a crippling car accident while under the influence. Yes, you want desperately to save her from these.

But most mistakes don't ruin a teenager's life—quite the contrary. When approached with the right mindset, they present opportunities for growth and can be transformative. Many good things can come from mistakes. They decrease self-righteousness, foster humility, and increase empathy. They also provide opportunities to take responsibility, learn forgiveness, and experience grace.

Your daughter can learn from her mistakes, and you want her making them at home while you can still guide her. You don't want her so controlled at home that she never learns how to monitor her own behavior. This sets her up to fail later in life.

If you feel conflicted and discouraged about your daughter's mistakes, then take thirty minutes and write out your feelings. It's important to clear out the fog of disappointment, frustration, and betrayal. Remember that your daughter is still growing. Teens make mistakes, and that's why she needs you. When the fog lifts you will be able to regain your clarity, without which you cannot discipline successfully.

Establishing Clarity in Your Home

Establishing clarity takes time and work, but it's well worth it. First, you need to evaluate the mistake, and get clear on what your daughter needs to learn. This informs what actions to take. Not only are you clear, but also you want your whole family to be clear about the rules, guidelines, and boundaries. Your daughter especially needs to be clear about any consequences beforehand.

Be Clear About What Your Daughter Needs Moms often get tripped up on the right way to handle their daughter's misbehaviors. It's not about how long you should ground your daughter. It's deeper than that. Your discipline is directly related to what she needs to learn. Your daughter's mistakes or negative behavior reveals where she is lacking insight, knowledge, and judgment. This determines what actions you take. The point of your discipline is to empower her with the life skills needed to live a successful life.

For example:

- If your daughter makes C's and D's in school, she needs *more structure and accountability* to get her work done.

- If she loses control and curses at you, she needs to learn *how to calm down.*

- If she throws her phone across the room and it breaks, she needs to *earn money to replace her phone.*

- If she drives home drunk from a party, she is *no longer allowed to drive.* When she starts driving again, she needs *more accountability.*

When your daughter makes a mistake, ask yourself this question. Does my daughter need:

- More structure and accountability?

- Stricter boundaries?

- Extra help and support?

- To take personal responsibility and make amends?

- To experience natural or logical consequences for her behavior?

- To learn how to calm down or slow down?

Ensure That Everyone Is Clear About Your Rules and Boundaries When raising a teenager you need to constantly evaluate your rules and boundaries. Responsibilities and routines regularly change, especially when your daughter gets her driver's license. Evaluate your current rules and boundaries by asking yourself the following questions:

- How is your daughter handling her current responsibilities?

- Are the boundaries in place protecting her?

- Is she able to flourish, or are my rules too constricting?

- Does she have enough autonomy to learn how to self-monitor and exhibit self-control?

- Does she have too much freedom?

If your daughter is flourishing, she can be rewarded with more autonomy. If she pushes the limits or is irresponsible, her independence needs to be reined in.

Once your rules and boundaries are clear to you, make sure your partner and daughter are on the same page. Make sure your daughter is clear and current about your expectations, rules, and boundaries. When there are changes, communicate them to your daughter when she is calm. You want them clear before the next opportunity presents itself.

And don't forget the siblings; unless she is an only child, your daughter does not live in a vacuum. Let the younger siblings know what rules they will face as they get older. Also you want to be clear with the siblings why the rules and boundaries differ for each child. If not, you will hear, "That's not fair" when one kid appears to have more privilege than their brother or sister.

Here's an example: Let's say a cute boy asks your fourteen-year-old daughter out. She has liked him for over a year. This is her dream come true. She comes to you begging, "Please, please, *please*, Mom, can we go out?" This is the time you want to remind her of your rules and boundaries, rather than initiating new ones. If they are not clear, your response may initiate a drama fest.

Even when you think you are clear, your daughter will look for loopholes, and you might be amazed at how clever this B minus student can be. You tell her, "I don't want you driving by yourself past midnight." She then stays out till 2:00 A.M. and says, "I thought it was okay because I wasn't by myself, I was with my boyfriend." If she finds a loophole, use this new information to redefine your rules and boundaries.

There Must Be Clear Consequences Not only does your daughter need to be clear about your rules and boundaries, she needs to be clear about what will happen if she breaks them. Prior knowledge will make it easier for you to implement the consequence. The fewer words said, the better. Avoid arguments. Gently remind her that she already knows the consequence. If your daughter is still angry, communicate to her through texting.

There are times the unexpected hits, and you don't know how to respond to her actions. You're not going to have your game plan down right away. It takes time to sort out what just happened. Seek out support from your partner and friends. It takes time to calm down, get clear, and process what she needs. You need this in order to execute an effective discipline.

You also want your daughter to be clear about *why* she is receiving the specific consequence. If she is upset, the reactive part of the brain is in control. She is offline from her higher brain, which would allow her to logically process what you said. Because of this, there's a strong chance she will misinterpret the point of the discipline. Let's say you found out your thirteen-year-old daughter is failing science. You tell her that she needs to be tutored once a week, and spend at least thirty minutes a day studying her science until her science grade improves. You think it's obvious *why* you set the limits, while she may think, "Mom's always mad at me. She's always picking on me." You need to communicate the obvious: "Look, you know you're a smart girl. You're just having some challenges with science. Meeting with a tutor once a week and studying for a half hour a day will help you to pass the course."

Your Potent Parenting Tools and How to Use Them

Now that you understand the purpose of empowered discipline and you're clear about what your daughter needs, you are ready to implement the discipline through one of the following Potent Parenting

Tools: learning conversations, employing impactful consequences, making amends, and depositing credit in the trust bank.

Your discipline can use one or more of these tools. Sometimes the learning conversation is all you need. In other situations, combine the learning conversation with one of the other three tools. Empowered discipline is not rigid. It's flexible, and you must be too. If the discipline is not getting the results you need, you can change the tool or your approach. Bottom line is that you want to use a tool that works for your daughter.

After you finish reading this chapter you can download your Potent Parenting Tools Worksheet at www.colleenogrady.com/book resources.

Learning Conversations

Since the root of *discipline* means "instruction given, teaching, learning, knowledge," then one of the best ways to do this is through the "learning conversation." Yes, you want to discipline behavior, but most importantly, if your daughter is truly going to learn, she has to own her mistake. A learning conversation is not a one-sided lecture by you. It's an authentic two-way conversation between you and your daughter. A learning conversation is successful when the timing is right, because only then will your daughter open up and receive your input without being defensive. There is an element of vulnerability between mother and daughter in the learning conversation. This opens the door for exploration and sharing real feelings, which helps your daughter see how her actions affect others and herself. She needs this to step out of her self-involvement (teens are quite naturally self-involved), develop empathy, and have a change of heart.

This may feel impossible to you. In the past, you've tried addressing issues with your daughter only to have her lie, get defensive, and overreact. It's maddening when you can't even have a conversation with your own daughter when she really needs it.

Don't give up yet. Learning conversations are possible when the timing is right. One reason it may not have worked for you if you've already tried it, or some form of it, is that you confronted her at the time of the incident, when emotions are at their highest. Remember that when you are emotionally flooded, the reactive brain takes over, making it biologically impossible to have any conversation. The key factor is to have the learning conversation when both of you are calm.

If you have an angry, defiant teen, you won't be able to have a learning conversation until her behavior is contained through a consequence. She needs to see that you are in charge and are taking her behavior seriously. Then, when she submits to the consequence, she is ready to have a conversation. For example, if your daughter takes her car out at night, breaking curfew, and her attitude is, "You can't tell me what to do," contain her behavior by taking away her car for the next two weeks. After not being able to drive her car for a week, she will be ready for the learning conversation—if for no other reason than she wants to get her car back.

A learning conversation is about maintaining a connection with your daughter even when there is conflict. And yes, it's challenging. She wants her independence and pushes your boundaries, and you need to reel her in and protect her. You may find that both of you are standing on opposite shores of a great divide. This can be a very painful and scary time for moms. But it's up to you to protect your relationship. You do this by building a bridge through empathic listening, curiosity, and understanding. You need this in order for your daughter to come clean.

This will be the hardest work you will ever do as a mom. It takes courage to truly listen to what's going on with your daughter. It's imperative that she come out of hiding. You want her to tell you the truth, even when you don't like what you hear. No mom wants to hear that her daughter has skipped school, smoked weed, had sex, or is pregnant. Every part of you wants to shut down or scream. But it's crucial that you stay present and not react. What can help you stay centered is to tell yourself, "She's going to be okay, and we will find a way through this."

When she feels you are truly listening, understanding, and genuinely care, she will be real with you. This is what you want. You also want to hear her thinking process, or lack of one. What information is she ignoring? How did she feel after the incident? Knowing this can help you accurately redirect her and give her the information she needs.

After you have listened to her story, it's your turn. Start with communicating understanding. Again, this builds a bridge. "I understand that you love your boyfriend." "I know that hanging out with your friends is important to you." When you communicate your understanding, your daughter is more apt to listen to you.

And here is where the learning occurs.

But first, let's revisit the undeveloped prefrontal cortex. Her undeveloped PFC is not thinking through long-term consequences and cause and effect. It tends to be impulsive. Also, remember the drive for the dopamine reward and hyperrational thinking. Your daughter is driven towards thrill seeking and romance and will downplay important facts. This is where you step in. You insert the missing or ignored information. You help her see the cause and effect and the long-term consequences. You connect the dots as to why you had to put the brakes on her risky behavior. You remind her that your job is to guide and protect her.

Another benefit of the learning conversation is that it can bring you closer. After all the tears and expressed emotions, everything is out in the open. The wall of hostility between you and your daughter is gone. This opens the door to love, forgiveness, and reconciliation.

Employing Impactful Consequences

It is important for teens to learn that their actions have consequences, both positive and negative. Teens, with their undeveloped prefrontal cortex, often miss the connection between their actions and the consequences that follow. Parents can teach their teens through both natural consequences and parental consequences. *Natural* consequences automatically happen to your daughter as a result of her actions. *Parental* consequences, also known as *logical* consequences, are constructed with the intent to instruct and guide. They are implemented when natural consequences are not effective or appropriate.

What makes natural and parental consequences impactful is that they can produce a shift in your daughter's mindset. She will start making the much-needed connections between cause and effect, and she will gain the missing or undeveloped life skills she needs. Because of these consequences, your daughter moves forward with more compassion, wisdom, and maturity than before her mistake.

Natural Consequences It's vital that your daughter owns her mistakes and takes responsibility for them. Integral to this is that she feels the discomfort of her choices. Natural consequences are great teachers, because it's how life works. If you touch a hot stove, you burn your hand—lesson learned. The consequences do the talking, and make your life easier. There is no need to argue with your daughter. You can be empathic and understanding, while the natural consequences teach her life's lessons.

For example, your daughter spends her weekly allowance by Thursday. She has no money to go to dinner with her friends on the weekend. This natural consequence works because it's immediate, and it feels bad. Your daughter has to feel the disappointment in order to learn the lesson. Next time she will budget her money.

The problem is that you can inadvertently sabotage natural consequences for the following reasons:

- You don't want your daughter to be unhappy.

- You don't want her to miss out on opportunities.

- You don't want her to have a bad reputation.

In the example above, if your daughter runs out of cash, she'd run straight to you and ask for more money. If you give her the money, you rob her of the natural consequences. What she learns instead is there's no need to budget her money because there's endless cash. This is an inaccurate picture of how adulthood works. When you interfere with natural consequences, your daughter's sense of entitlement and privilege increases while her sense of personal responsibility decreases. She will expect to be bailed out of tough situations and rewarded for her mistakes.

Your daughter must be aware that you won't always bail her out. There is nothing like a natural consequence to teach and motivate your daughter. She learns quickly that her success is based on taking responsibility for her actions.

Many times, there are natural consequences that are too dangerous to allow. For instance, if your daughter is drinking heavily and driving, you don't want her to experience the natural consequence of getting into an accident. It's dangerous and could be fatal for everyone involved.

You also don't want to use natural consequences when the results are too far off in the future. Your high school freshmen daughter who fails a course may not understand how this will impact her getting into a good college. She won't feel the pain of her actions until many years later.

When your daughters not safe and you need to protect her or when the natural consequences are not immediate you can use parental consequences.

Parental Consequences When you give a parental consequence you want to make sure that both parents are in agreement. An angry and upset teen brings chaos, drama, and confusion into the home. If you're not intentional, the stress will strain your relationship with your partner, and your daughter may use the tension to divide and conquer in order to get her way. If you say no, she will try to get her dad to say yes. This is why you want to keep your partner informed and current so you can be a united front.

Parental consequences are never angry or reactive responses; they are logical and directly related to what your daughter needs to learn. For them to be successful they need to be planned in advance and agreed upon by both parents. Your daughter also needs to give her input and agree to the consequence beforehand. Here are four questions that can help you create an effective consequence:

1. **Will the consequence be an effective teaching tool?** You want your consequence to be instructive instead of just a punishment. For example, if your daughter is making bad grades be-

cause she is doing everything but studying, a logical consequence is that she must do school work before watching TV, playing video games, and going out. This consequence is directly related to what your daughter needs. She must learn how to manage her time and delay gratification.

Big consequences, like grounding your daughter for a semester because of poor grades, can be counterproductive. It doesn't equip her with the life skills she needs. And she loses her motivation because there is no end in sight. Most likely, this consequence will result in an angry teen who is locked in her room and refusing to study

2. **Are you willing to do what it takes to enforce this consequence?** Logical consequences should be enforceable; don't create a consequence you can't enforce. If consequences are too demanding on your time or energy, you are likely not to follow through on them. For instance, if the consequence is that your daughter is grounded from driving her car for the rest of the semester, it may be too hard on you to enforce, especially if she is driving her sister to school every day and you work full-time. What you *could* enforce is that she can't use the car for anything but school or school-related activities.

3. **Can you be consistent with the consequences?** Make sure you follow through on your consequence, no matter how your daughter pushes you. If you are inconsistent, you lose your credibility. Your daughter will learn that if she makes enough of a fuss, you will change your mind. Your daughter needs to see the strength and actions behind your words. While she won't admit it, she will likely admire you for being firm.

You teach her (by modeling) how to set limits and boundaries. If she experiences you being consistent and strong, she will be much more likely to adhere to the boundaries you have set. For example, you tell your daughter that she needs to stay home this weekend and focus on her schoolwork because she is failing algebra. On Saturday she threatens to cut classes on

Monday and miss her algebra test if you don't let her go out with her friends. Reluctantly, you let her go. In this situation no one wins. Your daughter sees you as someone she can manipulate, and won't take you seriously next time you give her a consequence.

4. **Are you also willing to reward good behavior?** You want to be consistent, but not rigid. There are times you need to be flexible with the consequences and reward your daughter's positive behavior. When your daughter works hard at winning back your trust and you reward her efforts, she will be motivated to try harder. For instance, let's say your daughter was caught smoking weed. You won't let her hang out with her old friends because you now know they all use drugs. You tell your daughter that she needs to stay home for the next month. You also tell her to go to a recovery meeting and join an APG (alternative peer group) with other kids who are in recovery. She goes willingly and keeps attending the meetings. You start to see a change in her. You have a successful learning conversation. She opens up about how she started smoking weed and what other drugs she has used. She says she is serious about getting sober. Her new friends from her APG ask her to hang out on Friday night. Technically, she is still grounded, but you decide to let her go because you see such a change in her attitude and her behavior. You also want to reward her for hanging out with kids who are sober.

Making Amends

This is one of my favorite tools because it is all about your teen taking full responsibility for her actions. To make amends is to correct a mistake. It's about restoring what's been damaged, which is usually the connection between the two of you. There are many benefits to making amends. It allows for self-forgiveness, and releases guilt. In addition, your daughter learns that she has the power to make things right. Amends have a healing effect on both your daughter and on you.

There are three components to making amends: taking responsibility for an action, apologizing for that action, and identifying what must be done to make amends for the incident.

Taking Responsibility Part of your daughter's taking responsibility for her action is facing the reality of her impact on others. This helps develop empathy. Taking appropriate responsibility moves your daughter out of shame ("I'm a terrible person") or blaming others ("It's actually all *your* fault") to taking effective action. It empowers your daughter while fostering humility and authenticity.

Most teenage girls balk at taking personal responsibility and will justify their actions. One time, when my daughter was thirteen, she lost her temper, went into a rage, and said very inappropriate things to me. After she calmed down I told her she needed to take responsibility for her words and make it up to me. The next thing I know one of my dogs comes in the room with a rolled up piece of paper in its collar. It was a note from my daughter telling me she was sorry. But there was more. This was the beginning of a scavenger hunt through my house. At each destination she left me another note where she apologized for something else. The final destination was a list of everything she appreciated about me. This touched me deeply because she came up with this creative and heartfelt idea on her own. This took a lot of thought and energy. Her actions and affirming words made amends for her cruel and unwarranted words, and brought us closer together.

Apologizing Think of an apology as an exercise in good manners. Just as you can teach your daughter good manners, you can teach her how to give an appropriate apology so that she does the right thing, even if she doesn't feel like it.

Once your daughter calms down after an action and has time to reflect on what she did, ask her to give you an apology. She can give you one verbally, but my preference is that she write it out. In person she may say "I'm sorry" with an attitude or without thinking it through. Writing helps her reflect on her actions and see the effect she has on others.

Teach her how to write an apology by starting with "I'm sorry, Mom, for . . . ." Tell her to be specific. She needs to own her mistake and not blame it on anyone else. She needs to include in her apology how her actions impacted others and end with how she will make amends.

Making Amends First your daughter needs to identify what she will do to make amends and when she will implement it.

It is more powerful for both of you if your daughter comes up with how she will make up for her action on her own, and that you are not dictating what it is. Again this helps her take responsibility. It also works because it's her idea and it gives you one less thing to argue about. You can prompt her by telling her how the incident impacted you and everyone else in your family. Then you tell her she needs to demonstrate that she "gets it" by making a noble gesture to make it right. In most cases you'll be surprised and pleased by what your daughter will come up with. It's important that she gives you a deadline by which she will make her amends, and it needs to be made within the week.

There are some teens who aren't ready to make amends and won't take it seriously. If this is true then you can use parental consequences instead of amends or one of the other potent parenting tools,

Depositing Credit in the Trust Bank

The fourth Potent Parenting Tool involves rebuilding trust. Trust is what the parenting relationship is based on. You place your confidence in the character, ability, strength, and truthfulness of your daughter— and she, that you have her best interests at heart. Think of this as a Trust Bank. Every time your daughter shows herself to be trustworthy, she deposits credit in her Trust Bank. Trust must be earned.

Conversely, when your daughter lies and disregards your rules and boundaries, she drains the trust account and must earn your trust all over again.

Your daughter may promise you that she will never break your trust again and demand that you trust her. But you have no reason to, until her actions back it up. Let's say that you catch your fifteen-year-old daughter sexting with her boyfriend. You take away her phone and you find out she's been using your computer behind your back. Now the Trust Bank is completely overdrawn. Taking away her phone and computer is not the same as her earning trust back. The burden of proof is on her. She needs to begin making deposits. She starts with being open and forthcoming.

Examples of this are . . .

- She lets you look through her phone.

- She agrees to your talking to her boyfriend's parents.

- She complies with what you ask.

- She calls you from her friend's house and lets you talk to her friend's mom.

- She brings her friends over.

- She volunteers to get a drug test.

Trust goes both ways. You daughter needs to trust that you mean what you say, that you'll make good on your promises—consequences—and that you love her no matter what.

* * *

Your daughter's worst mistake doesn't define who she is or will be. Mistakes are a given for teens, considering their undeveloped brain. This is why she still lives at home. She needs your empowered discipline, which is to give instruction, knowledge, and to teach. Empowered discipline is not reactionary, but strategic and built on a foundation of clarity and the right mindset. You empower your daughter by giving her guidance through the first potent parenting tool, the learning conversation. The other three tools—employing impactful consequences, making amends, and depositing credit in the trust bank—equip her with life skills needed to be a successful adult. Empowered discipline can transform a mistake and turn it into an opportunity for growth and authenticity, and bring a closer connection with your daughter.

PART III

Creating a New Future for You and Your Daughter

CHAPTER 10

What Your Daughter Needs to Thrive

Rachel was doing her best as a single working mom. Widowed three years earlier, she was raising two teenage daughters. She recently came to the session with Hannah, her younger daughter.

Hannah had just started high school and was not doing well. Her grades had dropped, as had her self-confidence. Hannah was stressed because she was gaining weight and felt "ugly." In addition, her boyfriend had just dropped her and losing him made her miss her dad all over again. Hannah also felt lost in her new school. She knew one girl, but they had different lunch periods, so she ate alone every day.

When I asked Rachel how her daughter had been doing before starting high school, she said Hannah was fine. She had a good group of friends and was involved in lots of school activities.

It was clear that Hannah was having a difficult transition. There were a lot of issues to address, but first, I wanted to evaluate her nutrition, sleep, and exercise habits. These basic necessities can significantly impact your emotions and overall well-being.

I asked Hannah how much sleep she got on average each night. Though Rachel told me it was lights out at 10:00 P.M., Hannah said she was tired all the time. This didn't make any sense, so I asked if she had her phone by her side at night, and she admitted that she did. I also asked if she texted her friends at night, and reluctantly she said, "Sometimes." In fact, it turned out that she was texting her friends and her ex-boyfriend every night, sometimes until 3:00 A.M. No wonder she was tired. I told her she would feel significantly better if she got eight hours or more of uninterrupted sleep.

I then asked Hannah what she ate for breakfast. "Nothing," she answered. "I hate breakfast food." Her mom was shocked, because every morning she gave her a waffle wrapped in a paper towel. "I just throw it away when you're not looking," Hannah told her. "How about lunch?" I asked. "I don't like to bring a lunch, so I buy French fries in the cafeteria." Hannah would then come home from school starved, and binge on chips, cookies, and leftover pizza.

"How alert are you in your first period class?" I asked. "I can't stay awake," Hannah replied. "I often drink a double espresso at lunch to try to wake up." I told her she was missing the "brain foods," like protein or glucose, which give us the energy we need to pay attention.

"How about exercise?" I asked. Hannah told me she had quit dance because she wasn't any good. I explained why exercising regularly was imperative, and told her that "besides the obvious reasons, it reduces stress and gives you four 'I feel good' body chemicals—endorphins, dopamine, serotonin, and norepinephrine."

Hannah began feeling better when she started eating healthy meals, getting uninterrupted sleep, and exercising often. Now she had the energy to address her other issues. We wanted to get her connected at school, so we came up with a strategy to help Hannah find her tribe. We wanted to change her home environment as well. Mom admitted that she was worried about her daughter's grades and had been hard on Hannah. We determined that mom needed extra support. so we worked on building Team Hannah, which included a tutor. This allowed mom to lighten up and enjoy her daughter more.

When problems occur with your daughter, you can feel lost. This chapter helps you identify your daughter's core needs. With this information, you can build a framework that will protect her and help her thrive. This empowers you to act proactively and create a big picture parenting strategy. This chapter gives you a checklist to look at when something goes wrong. Working through this checklist gave Rachel a comprehensive game plan for Hannah, starting with the fundamentals of nutrition, sleep, and exercise. Other essential areas included a flourishing home environment, a place to belong, and a team of supportive adults. The good news is that sometimes there are simple, practical solutions that can turn around difficult situations.

The Fundamentals of Good Health: Nutrition, Sleep, and Exercise

A garden flourishes when it has the proper balance of all the elements; the same applies to your teenage daughter. Most of this is not news to you. You know that in order for your daughter to blossom, she needs to eat healthy, get plenty of sleep, and exercise regularly. But what often happens is that your daughter wears you down with her resistance and you resign yourself to her junk food diet, five hours of sleep, and lack of exercise.

Here's what you can do to get your daughter back on track.

Nutrition and Healthy Eating

The first step toward better nutrition and healthy eating should begin by convincing your daughter to stay away from simple sugars found in cookies, cakes, candy, and ice cream. They give a quick spike of energy but result in a quicker drop, which leads to emotional slumps and problems with concentration.

Your daughter needs a healthy diet to function at her best. It starts with a nutritious breakfast. She also needs to drink plenty of water, eat healthy snacks, and not skip meals.

You can make a huge difference in your teen's life by understanding that she needs glucose as fuel for her brain, but that the glucose must come from complex carbohydrates such as whole grains, nuts, vegetables, and fruits, not from refined sugar products. A steady supply of glucose keeps physical and emotional energy stable and helps your daughter concentrate and pay attention.

Your daughter also needs proteins, the brain's building blocks; they generate new brain cell connections and build new neural pathways. Protein changes into amino acids, which convert into neurotransmitters that carry messages from one brain cell to another. Foods high in protein include eggs, meat, fish, quinoa, and dairy products like milk, cheese, and yogurt.

The challenging part is getting your daughter on board. Moms, teenage girls, and food can be an explosive combination. Here's why. Your daughter's eating is erratic. Her undeveloped prefrontal cortex contributes to this, as evidenced by her poor impulse control, disconnection from cause and effect, and lack of concern about long-term consequences.

Does this sound familiar? You make her a good breakfast but she doesn't eat it. You watch her binge on anything that contains lots of sugar, salt, and fat. Then you hear her complaining, "I'm so fat, I hate myself."

So, because your daughter is crying her eyes out, you try to be helpful. You offer her some practical advice like, "Honey, you can lose that weight by eating healthy and taking small portions." Instead of saying, "Thanks, Mom," she leaves the room, slamming the door and muttering obscenities.

Why does she get so upset? What's really going on is shame. Girls flip through magazines of Photoshopped models and compare their bodies to this unattainable ideal. Because of the culture we live in, girls feel pressured to have the perfect body, and become critical of their own. This is why eating disorders are so prevalent in teen girls. According to the National Association of Anorexia Nervosa and Associated Disorders, 95 percent of those who have eating disorders are between the ages of twelve and twenty-five. Even girls who don't have eating disorders are extremely sensitive about their weight and body image. Their inner Mean Voice is telling them, "I'm too fat (or too skinny)." "I don't have a big enough thigh gap." "My breasts are too small or (rarely) too big." "My nose is too big (or too pointy)." "My hair is too curly (or too straight)." Name a body part, she can hate it. Knowing what is going on under your daughter's fiery facade will help you be more compassionate and patient with your daughter.

Here's what you can do:

- Educate your daughter about the benefits of a healthy diet, especially how it impacts her brain.

- Keep the refrigerator stocked with healthy snacks like fruits and vegetables. Keep binge foods like chips, cookies, and candy out of the house except for special occasions.

- Model healthy eating.

- Have an attitude of compassion, not criticism, toward her eating habits.

- Create a safe atmosphere for her to share her feelings.

- Avoid power struggles over food, particularly at meal times.

- Give her positive feedback for eating healthy rather than for being skinny.

If you are concerned that your daughter has an eating disorder, get professional help. A dietician can help her create a healthy food plan and gets you out of the power struggle. A licensed therapist can help her work through any emotional issues regarding food.

Before we leave this topic, I want to add a note about the not-uncommon reality of some teenage daughters becoming vegetarians, or even more difficult, vegans. No eye-rolling, please. They are maybe doing it just a little tiny bit to make your life more difficult, but they are more likely motivated by not wanting to hurt the animals or for health reasons. If she decides that she is a vegan, you not only want to listen why she has made this decision, you want to make sure she is meeting her nutrition needs, especially getting enough protein. Make sure you monitor her weight. If she is losing weight and she is adamant about being a vegan, take her to a reputable dietician.

A Good Night's Sleep

It's hard for a teenage girl to get enough sleep. You tell your daughter it's time for bed but she says she needs to study for her history test. This may pose a dilemma. You may feel you have to choose between your daughter's getting a good night's sleep or passing her test, and most often sleep loses. This is because many of our teens have schedules packed with afterschool activities. This causes their homework and social life to get pushed back into the late-night hours and has produced a culture of sleep-deprived teens.

Sleep deprivation has many negative consequences. First, it decreases serotonin, one of the "feel-good" chemicals in the brain, and increases the stress hormone cortisol, which in turn increases mood volatility. This leads to mood swings, irritability, and depression that create over-the-top reactions to situations. James E. Gangwisch and his colleagues from Columbia University, College of Physicians and Surgeons, Department of Psychiatry, found that teenagers who routinely went to bed after midnight were 24 percent more likely to be depressed than those who got to sleep by 10:00 P.M. or earlier. They also found that teenagers who regularly sleep five or fewer hours are 71 percent more likely to report depression

Sleep deprivation affects school performance as well. It impairs the functioning memory, which results in your daughter forgetting her assignments and keeps her from retaining what she's learned. It's hard to focus, reason, learn, create, or perform when you are sleep deprived.

Sleep deprivation is exacerbated by big changes in sleep patterns brought on by puberty. Have you noticed that your daughter is wide awake at 11:00 P.M. when you are struggling to keep your eyes open? The timing of the sleep/wake cycle is different for teens. Though scientists are not sure why, the brain secretes the hormone melatonin later in the day in teens, which translates to being wide-awake at midnight and dead tired in the morning. When you combine the shift in the sleep cycle with their busy schedules, it's no surprise that the average teen gets only six or seven hours of sleep a night. The truth is, however, that they need nine to ten hours of sleep for their brains to regenerate and operate at peak efficiency. Plus, the teen brain needs time to sort out and process all the neural connections built up during the day.

Here's what you can do:

- Convince your daughter to calm down before bedtime. Unplug from electronics— including cell phones, video games, TV, and chatting on the computer—an hour before bed. Scientists have found that pulsed microwave radiation from cell phones causes the brain to switch to alpha waves, and this is not conducive to sleep. Have her try quieter activities instead, like reading a book, listening to relaxing music, or writing in her journal.

- Monitor her cell phone and computer use. Take her phone and laptop at night so she won't be tempted to chat with her friends, especially if she is a younger teen.

- Eliminate caffeine and sugar beverages from her nighttime diet. It takes three to five hours to get rid of half of the effects of caffeine and fourteen hours to process all of it.

- Let her sleep in on the weekend to catch up on her rest.

- Educate your daughter about sleep deprivation and the benefits of sleep.

Regular Exercise

Current trends show that teens exercise less and sit more, due to screen time of their choosing (Internet, Facebook, and TV)—and to demanding homework. There is another reason for decreased exercise. Girls will quit dance, swim team, volleyball, track, and gymnastics if they feel they can't compete with the top athletes. Girls have associated exercise with competition, and when that's the case they often give up exercise because they're "not good enough."

This has to be turned around. Exercise is critical for all of us, but especially for teens. It's essential for their physical, mental, and emotional health. There are many benefits to exercise beyond being in shape.

Exercise not only strengthens muscles, but it builds better brains. Recent studies show that forty minutes of vigorous exercise a day helps teens better organize their schoolwork and improve their performance in the classroom. Exercise generates more brain activity in the prefrontal cortex, which helps teens with their working memory and planning. It also helps them stay alert and focused.

Exercise gives teens a natural high by increasing the four feel-good body chemicals. Most everyone has heard of the runner's high, caused by endorphins, the neurotransmitters linked to happiness and elevated mood. But they also found that when the heart is pumping strongly, it increases the amounts of those other three neurotransmitters, dopamine, serotonin, and norepinephrine. Dopamine is going to make your daughter feel happier and more optimistic. Serotonin helps stabilize her mood, which helps her relax, and reduces negativity and aggression. Norepinephrine gives the energy boost needed to better focus and store and recall memory.

Exercise also relieves pressure and decreases stress. A thirty-minute cardio workout gets rid of the excess adrenaline and cortisol in the body for twenty-four hours! In other words, exercise rids the body of the tension and anxiety immediately, enabling your daughter to calm down and function at her best.

Here's what you can do:

- Have your daughter start small by walking the dog around the block.

- Help her bring back the fun in exercise. Take a group of friends roller-skating.

- Make it easy for her. Give her a membership to the local YMCA.

- Help her think outside the box by trying a Zumba class, ice-skating, or water-skiing.

- Encourage her to diversify. If she has only done team sports she can try individual sports. Also, besides cardio she can work on flexibility and balance by learning tae kwon do or yoga.

- Encourage your daughter to combine socializing with exercise by going to the gym with a friend.

- Suggest that she remove the stress of competition by swimming on her own, not on a swim team.

- Educate her about the benefits of thirty to forty minutes of cardio a day. I found girls get motivated when they realize that exercise decreases stress and helps them feel good.

A Flourishing Home Environment

How would you describe the environment in your home? Would you say it's peaceful, structured, playful, supportive, and encouraging? Or would you say it's tense, stressful, and nonstop drama. No family is 100 percent blissful. However, the dominant feeling of your home affects everyone in your family. A stress-filled environment robs your family of peace, joy, love, creativity, rest, and security. A flourishing home environment is intentional and deliberate. You need this to dial down the drama and build a supportive atmosphere.

Dial Down the Drama

A stress-filled environment breeds drama. Random House Dictionary defines stress as "physical, mental, or emotional strain or tension." When you have tension, worry, and stress, you are going to have drama. The opposite is also true: Drama breeds stress. They are so closely related you need a plan to decrease stress and eliminate drama.

Decrease Stress One practical way to decrease stress is to make sure you have downtime in your schedule. Downtime is a pressure-free zone. It allows families to slow down, relax, play, rest, and enjoy each other's company. Your daughter definitely needs this. Downtime allows her to let go of the stress caused by friends, grades, chores, and parental expectations. It allows family members to de-stress and create positive experiences with each other. It is where the positive memories come from.

Downtime is not only good for reducing stress, it's good for your daughter's active teenage brain. Dr. Michael Rich of Harvard Medical School and executive director of the Center on Media and Child Health in Boston has said, "Downtime is to the brain what sleep is to the body." Downtime allows your daughter's brain to rest and keeps her from feeling overwhelmed. Like sleep, downtime helps the brain to operate at peak efficiency by allowing it time to process all the new neural connections. Downtime allows the brain to replenish. A brain that has had time to rest can naturally restore attention, motivation, and creativity. When you see your daughter zoning out in front of the TV, know this is not wasted time.

Downtime just doesn't happen; you have to schedule it. When you're scheduling activities, make sure you factor in time to relax.

Downtime needs to be balanced with organization and structure, because too much downtime can create stress. You'll learn how systems and structures will make your life run smoothly in the next chapter.

Here's how you can reduce stress in your home. First, get your family on board by discussing how stress impacts them. Steer clear of blame or rehashing past dramas. Focus on the general characterization like, "Everyone is more on edge." Because one person's stress impacts everyone else, each family member needs to take responsibility. Try having everyone name one thing they will do to reduce stress. For example:

- I'll take the evening off.

- I'll exercise before I come home from work.

- I'll drop out of one activity.

- I'll organize my room.

- I'll write in my journal for twenty minutes.

Or have them say what they *need* to reduce their stress.

- I need to listen to my music on the way to school.

- I need thirty minutes after school to wind down before I start my homework.

- I need you to ask me a day ahead of time if you need something from the store.

- I need to work out for an hour after work.

Eliminate Drama   Eliminate drama with a "no-drama policy." This is one of the best ways to reduce stress. Drama includes yelling, name calling, shaming, using vulgar language, threatening, door slamming, pushing, hitting, or breaking things. A no-drama policy establishes emotional and physical safety in your home.

Start with getting your partner to agree to this policy. Next, invite your family to participate. Though teenage girls are often the instigators, they will likely agree to the policy. They don't like to be yelled at either.

A no-drama policy means everyone is responsible for maintaining self-control and calming themselves down as necessary. Each family member needs to identify their strategy for this, be it listening to music, praying, meditating, talking to friends, going for a run, going to the gym, reading a book—or even puttering in the kitchen or garage.

Create a Family Intention

Now that you have your no-drama policy in place, it's time to create a new vision for your family. You do this by creating a "family intention." This includes what both you *and* your family members want. A family intention steers the focus away from what's wrong and toward imagining what's possible. What would your home look like without stress and drama? How would a flourishing home environment feel? Family members may each answer these questions differently, especially your daughter.

Your daughter will likely want a "teen-friendly" home, which is more about the environment than having an Olympic-sized swimming pool. The atmosphere in a teen-friendly home is warm, welcoming, and relaxed. Her friends would feel free to lounge around, raid your refrigerator, laugh loudly, play their music, and have fun. If the house feels tense, they won't want to hang out.

Each family member needs to contribute to create a family intention. You want everyone to own it. Here are three questions that will help you create a family intention.

1. What's one word to describe your ideal home? (*Sample responses:* peaceful, positive, safe, warm, respectful, fun, loving, connected, playful, organized, relaxing)

2. How would family members treat each other if you had a flourishing home environment? (*Sample response:* "They would be encouraging and understanding, rather than yelling or losing their tempers.")

3. What is something that you do want in your ideal home? (*Sample response:* "I want to be able to come home from school and relax.")

Now combine everyone's answers together and create your intention. Your family intention can be as simple as, "Our home is respectful, fun, relaxed, and caring." What's great about this is that your entire family has bought into it. Write it down and place it on the refrigerator so that everyone can see it. Your family intention is a reminder of what's really important and how family members should treat each other. This anchors the family when the stressful times come.

Build a Supportive Atmosphere

In a supportive atmosphere your daughter walks in the room and your face lights up. In a critical atmosphere, she walks into the room and you notice her dress is too short, her makeup too heavy and her hair's a mess. In other words, you see the negative immediately. You may not say anything, but she can read your face. She can tell if you are pleased or not. This negative response is a reactive one. You have a choice of having such a response, or having a more thoughtful response.

The reactive verbal response confronts quickly, and intensely. "Your room is disgusting." "You have on too much eyeliner." "Pull down your skirt." There is nothing wrong with what you're saying, but it's a good idea to not say anything immediately. Here's why. Her appearance has triggered strong emotions in you. It's not just that she has too much eyeliner or she is wearing a short skirt, it's where your imagination goes. You don't want her to look like a slut, nor do you want the other mothers to perceive her that way. So your reaction can be harsh. She, in turn, is not reacting as much to what you are saying but to the intensity of your tone, and the look of distaste on your face. Your daughter will not hear anything constructive out of that exchange, and will definitely not feel encouraged. She will feel criticized, even if you think you are helping her.

There are times she needs those direct responses, but if you are constantly correcting her and pointing out what she's doing wrong, you are not creating a supportive atmosphere. When your daughter feels constantly belittled, she will start avoiding you. If you are going to have a supportive atmosphere, encouragement, praise, and gratitude need to far outweigh the "helpful" criticism.

Your daughter needs you to be a thoughtful encourager. Words can help build her self-esteem or tear it down. You can intentionally build her confidence at home through complimenting her efforts, skills, and character. She needs this if she is to deal with turbulent teen relationships.

Being a thoughtful encourager does not happen automatically. It takes time to reflect and craft an encouraging response. "You have beautiful eyes, dear. You can go lighter on the eyeliner." You can disguise criticism with humor. "Your room is a jungle. There could be a family of squirrels and other animals living in there." She won't get defensive because you're not directly attacking her. Since the statement is absurd, she'll think it's funny.

Pointing out your daughter's negative behavior feels instinctive, but really it's a habit. Decide today to be a thoughtful encourager. Challenge yourself to say one encouraging thing a day to every member of your family. When you take the lead, your family will follow suit. When the overall atmosphere is supportive, you'll find that it is much easier to redirect her.

Here's what you can do to offer helpful praise and encouragement:

- Praise the effort rather than the underlying ability.

- Be specific with your praise, not general.

- Be sincere in your praise—or say nothing at all.

- Don't overdo the praise; you will sound phony.

A Place to Belong

A flourishing home environment is your daughter's safe harbor as she navigates her way into the teen culture. The world of teens is far from stable and many times is harsh and judgmental. Most of her energy is directed towards finding her BFF, boyfriend, and her group. She also needs a place to belong, in or out of school—whether it is as part of a soccer team or band, tennis club or art lessons—a place where she *feels* like she belongs. This sense of belonging is essential to your daughter's well-being.

The number one priority of a teenage girl is her relationships with her peers. This is why your daughter would rather hang out with her friends than do her homework. Her peers have a huge influence over her life. The way teenagers survive the transition from adolescence to adulthood is through their peer group. Your daughter cares deeply about what they think about her. Her greatest source of stress and suffering is feeling excluded and that no one cares about her. This is because she is wired to belong.

This feeling of belonging is challenging for adults, and can be vicious for teenage girls. I have observed girls' politics for decades. I remember what it felt like when I was a teen, and I have seen it with my teenage daughter. For ten years I observed teens in high school cafeterias, at football games, and on twenty-four-hour bus trips. I watched girls reject friend after friend when a more popular girl approached. Girls can be mean, critical, self-centered, flaky, judgmental, and unforgiving. Being ridiculed by her peers will damage your daughter's self-esteem. School can feel like a battle zone.

Girls know when they belong. It feels comfortable. They feel accepted and can be themselves. Girls also know when they *don't* belong. It feels bad. They feel on edge and tense. If your daughter doesn't feel like she belongs, it's a really big deal to her. She is not being a drama queen. Your daughter needs you to listen to her. She needs a safe place to talk about her feelings. These feelings can be intense and severe, and need to be soothed. For twenty-five years as a marriage and family therapist, I have seen what can happen to girls. If they feel like they don't matter, they cut themselves, have suicidal thoughts, numb out with drugs and alcohol, act out sexually, or become anxious and depressed. What do you get when you combine a bunch of reactive teenage brains in a highly competitive environment? A lot of hurt feelings.

You can see why peer pressure exists, when you consider the desperate need to fit in and the enormous need for approval. This is why your daughter gets so upset if her hair doesn't look right or she's wearing the wrong clothes. She's afraid she'll be rejected and ostracized. It's one thing to have peer pressure to wear a certain pair of shoes, but it can also put your daughter at risk. If she has to choose connection over compromising her values, she will pick connection.

Our daughters must be educated about what it truly means to belong. It's more than being popular. Being popular is more about ranking than connection. In her book *Gifts of Imperfection,* Brené Brown tells us that "Love belongs with belonging . . . I can't separate the concepts of love and belonging because when [my clients] spoke of one, they always talked about the other." This is what girls need to learn and practice.

Here's what you can do to help your daughter feel she belongs:

- **Show unconditional love and belonging at home.** She needs to know that she is worthy of love and belonging. She learns this by *experiencing* it. This starts at home in all the myriads of interactions she has with you and other members of your family. Your daughter will pick up on how you feel about her. If your daughter feels your acceptance and unconditional love, instead of judgment and criticism, she can relax and be herself. You have given her a safe place to assert her emerging personality. When she experiences that you enjoy who she truly is, she knows she is worthy of belonging.

- **Listen and validate her feelings.** It's important to listen to your daughter's stories and validate her feelings. With all of her drama queen language it can be hard to take her seriously. When you hear her say, "Mom, they are so mean and rude. They hate me," this is when it's easy to dismiss her story by saying, "They don't hate you!" This contradicts her feelings rather than validating them. Instead, ask her to tell you more. Be compassionate. Listen to her stories through the teenage lens. Remember what your high school experience was like. Tell her things like, "That must have really hurt," or "That must have been embarrassing." If she feels you understand and care, she will tell you more and you will get a clear idea of what is going on in her life.

- **Bring back the Golden Rule.** Your daughter needs to learn that if you want someone to be nice, kind, and respectful to you, you need to treat others the same. In this culture, girls are extremely competitive and try to one-up each other. This doesn't make for good friendships. They need to be taught the Golden Rule: Do to others as you would have them do to you. You have to help them make that connection: If they want to have a good friend, they have to *be* a good friend to others.

- **Facilitate teenage "play dates."** It can be so frustrating when you find a great youth group, dance class, or sports team and your daughter refuses to participate, or goes once and won't go back. The main reason is usually that she feels she doesn't belong. This is especially true of shy or introverted girls, who need to connect to one or a few girls before they are comfortable with a large group. One solution to this is to invite one of the girls over to the house. Take them to the beach, bowling, movies, shopping, or a concert. When your daughter feels comfortable with one, she will feel like she can tackle the group.

- **Find positive places for your daughter to belong.** Help your daughter by finding activities that will develop her skill and provide her a place to belong. This is well worth the time of shuttling kids and investing your money. Invest in group lessons in art, theatre, or dance. There are afterschool activities and school trips. There are summer camps that cover a wide range of interests, from sports and robotics to rock-and-roll. There are youth groups, girl scouts, and national charity leagues that do service projects in the community or worldwide. There are alternative peer groups that provide a safe and sober place for those teens in recovery. There is one important factor that will determine if a group is going to be positive or negative and that is determined by the adults leading it. You want to make sure your daughter is in a group led by healthy, supportive, and qualified adults.

A Team of Supportive Adults

Here's the good news. It's not all on you. Other adults can encourage, motivate, instruct, and give your daughter guidance. You can build a Daughter Team. Think of yourself as the CEO of your daughter's well-being. You can oversee everything concerning your daughter, but you don't have to do everything yourself. Evaluate what your daughter needs and then create an all-star team to support her.

Besides inspiring, supporting, instructing, and challenging your daughter, your Daughter Team provides a positive, consistent, and safe place to belong. You'll feel a huge relief when you intentionally create it and know you have your dream team in place.

Here is how to build your Daughter's Team:

1. **Start with evaluating your daughter's needs.** Remember, it's not all on you.

- Where do you need support concerning your daughter?

- Who are positive role models and who are not?

- Where does your daughter need help and support?

- Describe your daughter's dream team.

2. **Intentionally spend time with your extended family.** Identify the positive role models in your family and deliberately spend time with them. This includes grandparents, partners, stepparents, family friends, nephews, nieces, brothers, sisters, uncles, and aunts. You want your daughter hanging out with as many positive family members as possible. Have regular multigenerational family gatherings, not just at Thanksgiving. This gives teens a safe place to belong without peer pressure.

3. **Surround your daughters with other positive role models.** A teenage girl spends a majority of time at school and other activities. Make sure there are positive adults who will love, support, challenge, and encourage her. Teachers, coaches, tutors, directors, instructors, mentors, and even youth ministers can change the course of a teen's life in a positive or destructive way. Your daughter will experience plenty of annoying teachers, but beware of instructors who use abusive and shaming tactics. Many girls have given up on their dreams because of harsh, condescending instructors. A teenage girl can only thrive when she feels physically and emotionally safe. These same girls who quit would have flourished with positive and nurturing instructors. Know the adults who are in your daughter's life. Meet with the teachers. Observe a basketball practice or dance class. You may think your daughter is exaggerating, but she may be telling you the truth. If your daughter is losing her confidence, it may be time to take action.

4. **Get professional help as needed.** There are times your daughter may need professional help. Don't hesitate to get it if she is suffering from severe depression, anxiety, loss, trauma, eat-

ing disorders, or drug and alcohol abuse. This can be a frightening time for parents, and especially scary when you can't help her directly. In these times, you help her by connecting her to the right professional, be it a dietician, a life coach, or licensed therapist.

* * *

You don't have to wait for the other shoe to drop; you can be a proactive positive force in your daughter's life. I've provided a blueprint for your daughter to thrive by giving you the big picture strategy instead of focusing on the drama of the day. You can also download your How to Help Your Daughter Thrive Worksheet at www.colleen ogrady.com/bookresource to help you pinpoint problem areas when your daughter is not blossoming. Start with the basics of nutrition, sleep, and exercise. Work on creating a flourishing home environment—this will build her self-esteem and confidence. Help her find her place to belong with her teenage peers, and surround your daughter with a team of supportive coaches, mentors, and instructors. You don't have to do it alone.

CHAPTER 11

How to Recapture Your Life

Elizabeth is a stay-at-home mom. Before kids, she worked full-time and was a successful CPA, but she decided to quit when Samantha was born. She was grateful that her husband's income allowed her to stay home. Her oldest child, Morgan, was now a sophomore in college and was doing quite well. Samantha, a sixteen-year-old junior in high school, was a problem.

Elizabeth came to see me because she was constantly worried about Samantha. It seemed like something was always happening. One week, Elizabeth found weed and an empty wine bottle in her car after Samantha had borrowed it. A couple weeks later, she learned her daughter had lied about her friend Jasmine's parents being home during a sleepover when they actually were out of town. A few weeks after that, Elizabeth caught Samantha sneaking out of the house in the middle of the night to see her boyfriend.

Elizabeth was a devoted mom. She would make Samantha breakfast every morning and dinner every night, and she volunteered at her daughter's high school. But Samantha was spending less time at home because of her busy social calendar. Even when she was home, she would be in her room, door closed, talking to her friends. This hurt Elizabeth's feelings. She was both worried about Samantha and felt rejected by her.

I helped Mom work through her issues with Samantha, but there was something else going on. Elizabeth was so focused on her daughter that she had completely forgotten her own well-being. I asked Elizabeth how she took care of herself and she said, "I don't have time." I asked her, "What's one thing you'd like to do for yourself?" She said, "I'd love to sit down and read for thirty minutes a day, but I'd feel too guilty."

Elizabeth was neither loving being a mom nor enjoying her life. Being 100 percent focused on Samantha wasn't doing either of them any good. I wanted to help Elizabeth recapture the life she once loved.

Elizabeth's first priority was to protect, nurture, and guide her daughter. But when Elizabeth evaluated where she spent her time, she realized that most of it was spent *worrying* about Samantha, not protecting, nurturing, or guiding her. When she identified her other priorities, she realized that she'd been neglecting most of them, whether it was taking care of herself or spending quality time with her family and friends. Elizabeth soon discovered that she could begin enjoying her life again simply by getting her priorities straight and eliminating time wasters, like worry.

Your daughter's dramas can be so all-consuming that you lose touch with yourself. This chapter gives you practical ways to recapture your life, taking back all the important parts of you that make you healthy and happy. To do this, you need to regain control over your time and schedule, and not let the daily demands from your family run your life. Recapturing your life begins by identifying your priorities. No one else can do this for you. You are in charge of your own life.

Another step is clearing unnecessary and unwanted items from your plate, including clutter, chaos, and false obligations. Once you've cleared your plate, you're ready to schedule the life you want by getting your core needs in your schedule.

Prioritize the Life You Want

As a mom your life is busy; you don't have a lot of spare time. You start your day bright and early and run nonstop until bedtime. But a busy life is not necessarily a well-lived life, nor even a productive one. Your day is filled with lots of tasks and activities that vary in value and significance. It's up to you to determine what's really important and reflect that in your schedule. At the end of the day, when your head hits the pillow, you want to feel good about what you've accomplished. You don't want to be up all night worrying about what hasn't been done.

You may feel that you're too overwhelmed to think about priorities, that you don't have time to strategize. You're responding and reacting to everyone else's wants and needs, and as a result you aren't in control of your own life. If you're going to recapture the life you love, you need to get your priorities straight.

For some of you, prioritizing the life you want may sound selfish. Consider this: You are modeling what adulthood is like to your daughter. When you're enjoying your life, you make adulthood look attractive to her. When she sees you unhappy, upset, or worried, motherhood may not look too appealing. You want to model a life that is rich in relationships, responsibility, relaxation, and rewards. And the way you do this is by being the CEO of your own life.

Be the CEO of Your Own Life

Being the CEO of your own life means that you are in control, that you take complete responsibility for your own happiness and success. You stop blaming your daughter, partner, or parents for feeling unfulfilled. Remember Powerful Parenting Message #1 in Chapter 1, "It's crucial to pay attention to me." When you're in charge of your life, you have *permission* to invest in yourself. You don't need to question it anymore. You recognize that if your family is going to run successfully, you need to be functioning at your best.

It's important to believe that you are in control rather than a *victim* of circumstances. This is what happened to one of my clients,

Helen. She felt so powerless to change her situation with her kids, husband, and finances that she felt suicidal. Once Helen understood that she truly was the CEO of her own life, the hope returned, and she immediately had several good ideas to turn her situation around.

You can get stuck in the emotionality of your life, and that's when it's easy to feel like a victim. Feelings of hopelessness, anger, resentment, fear, and sadness can take over. Being your own CEO means that you honor and acknowledge your emotions, but you don't let them run your life. You provide emotional nurturance to your family and balance it with more left-brain functions that take a more practical and logical approach. These skills and strategies enable you to move forward and re-create the life you love.

A good CEO Mom takes time to evaluate her life through questions like:

- "What's working and what's not working?"

- "Am I taking care of myself?"

- "How can my family run more smoothly?"

- "Where am I spending my time?"

- "Is my schedule aligned with my priorities?"

As the CEO of your life, your chief responsibility is to make sure your priorities match up with how you spend your time. And we have a tool that helps you do just that.

Using the Priority Pie Assessment Tool

If you find yourself saying, "I have too much on my plate," you no doubt have a lot of work to do, plenty of problems to deal with, and way too many commitments.

A Priority Pie helps you assess what's on your plate and how you spend your time—and what's important to you—by dividing your activities into four quadrants: important and energizing, important and draining, normal everyday tasks, and time wasters.

The Priority Pie

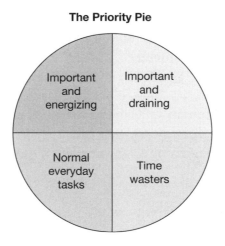

Important and Energizing In The first quadrant is everything in your life that is important to you. This could be anything from going running every day to taking a vacation with your husband. When you are doing things in this quadrant, you feel energized and fully alive. When you are taking action in this quadrant, you feel like you're living your purpose. You enjoy and look forward to these activities. They bring you positive emotions like joy, gratitude, happiness, delight, and love. They replenish your blessings. Though some are challenging, they're invigorating as well because you're using your unique gifts and abilities. At the end of your life, you are thankful for everything in this quadrant.

Important and energizing activities might include:

- Going out to eat with my daughter

- Spending time writing

- Starting my own business

- Having a long lunch with my best friend

- Playing the piano

Important and Draining The second quadrant contains the important and draining things you do. You know they have value and that your time is making a difference. Though they are draining, you are not resentful. You are grateful that you can contribute. You may not feel the rewards now, but they come later. Much of our parenting responsibilities fall into this category, such as having the learning or calm-down conversations with your daughter.

Important and draining activities might include:

- Doing the bookkeeping at my husband's business

- Driving my daughter to band rehearsal every day

- Helping my daughter with her homework

- Having my parents over for Sunday dinner

- Spending time with a family member who is in the hospital

Normal Everyday Tasks In the third quadrant are all the menial tasks that need to be done to run a household. While these tasks are necessary, they are not memorable. There are the repetitive daily duties like cooking, running the dishwasher, picking clothes off the floor, and running errands like going to the cleaners or making a deposit at the bank. These tasks are what fill up your to-do list.

Normal everyday tasks include:

- Paying bills

- Making doctors' appointments

- Cleaning the house

- Getting the oil changed in the car

- Doing the laundry

Time Wasters The fourth quadrant contains everything that squanders your time, whether it's spending two hours looking at pictures on Facebook or watching shows on Netflix till midnight. Time wasters don't replenish your energy or give you any real satisfaction.

Time wasters might include:

- Surfing the Internet

- Being on the phone all day complaining about your daughter

- Playing games on your iPad

- Checking your iPhone constantly

- Shopping for another purse

Now it's your turn. Write out everything you do in each of the four categories. Don't leave anything out. Now evaluate where you are spending the majority of your time. If you're spending most of your time in the bottom half of the Priority Pie, your priorities are going to be upside down, which is why you're not living the life you love. When more of your activities are in the top half of the Priority Pie, especially the first quadrant, you are content, energized, and enjoying your life, doing what you feel is important to you.

Moms typically spend the majority of their time doing normal everyday tasks and spend the least amount of time doing important and energizing activities. But now that you are the CEO of your life, you can do something about it. Let's reevaluate each quadrant.

- **Important and energizing:** The goal is to increase your time in first-quadrant activities, because these are your priorities. One priority may be "spending quality time with my daughter," but you need to be clear and specific about what quality time means for the two of you. For one mom, going shopping with her daughter is quality time; for you it might be hanging out in her room.

    Now quantify this time. How often do you want this quality time? If you said every day, how many minutes? Then, once you feel you have finished your list, ask yourself, "What's missing in this quadrant? What do I need to add to this list? Where do I need to clarify?"

- **Important and draining:** This second quadrant deserves some careful consideration. You need to take a hard look at the activities in this quadrant, asking yourself, "Do I need to be doing this?" Perhaps in this quadrant you have written, "Doing volunteer work at school." Now you must determine if you're doing the volunteer work that really matters to you and truly uses your gifts. Or are you just stuffing envelopes with notices that don't interest you? What can you eliminate in this quadrant? You may need to learn the art of saying no. Just because something is important, doesn't mean you should do it. Make sure you are using your unique abilities. For example, maybe you should be working on that short story you've been wanting to write. If your volunteer work is not an absolute yes, then say no.

  Caring for an ill family member is draining but very important. But you can still decide how much time you can give. These are hard decisions, but crucial for you and your family.

- **Normal everyday tasks:** The goal for your third-quadrant activities is to get some of these to-do items off your list. It may be hard for you to let go of anything. You want your cabinets, drawers, closets, and refrigerator to be organized in a specific way. You're afraid to let someone grocery-shop for you because they won't buy the right produce. What you need to consider is whether this may be keeping you from the things that really matter to you. Now, what can you let go of?

- **Time wasters:** The fourth quadrant is the most obvious place to recover your time. Eliminating time wasters can increase your time significantly. In actuality, time wasters are often more about being unconscious than enjoying the activity itself. For example, watching TV can be a great way to relax and is a nice reward after working hard. The key is that you must *define* your time, that is, consciously choose how much of it you are going to spend, and when—for example, "I'm going to watch a movie after I pay the bills." It's when your time is undefined that it gets wasted. Make a list of your time wasters. What activities do you need to be conscious of or define, and what activities can you eliminate?

Clear Your Plate for What's Important

It's time to get things off your plate so you can spend more in the top half of your Priority Pie. We've discussed how clearing your plate can involve saying no to *good* activities (stuffing envelopes at your daughter's school) to make room for the *best* activities (finally making the time to get back to your college love, creative writing). These are the hard choices you make; saying no means you might have to disappoint someone. This is hard for moms who have the "disease to please," but as CEO of your own life, your responsibility is to protect what's important to you and your family.

There are other ways to clear your plate that are more intangible, like eliminating clutter and chaos from your home, getting rid of false obligations, and asking for help.

Eliminate the Clutter and Chaos from Your Home

A cluttered and chaotic home reflects a cluttered and chaotic life. You can start decreasing the clutter and chaos in your life by decluttering your living space and restoring order.

Declutter Your Living Space By the time your daughter is a teenager you have accumulated a great deal of stuff, from her first-grade drawings and old Barbie dolls to closets packed with old clothes and toys. Add to this the rest of your family's possessions. After a while you can be so acclimated to the clutter that you are blind to it.

Clutter drains your energy and spoils your mood. Decluttering can be hopeful. You are literally releasing baggage from your past. Decluttering is a relatively easy way to take charge of your life, see positive change, and move forward. Getting rid of stacks of papers or ten-year-old T-shirts is much easier than dealing with an angry or unhappy (probably both) teenage girl.

When you get rid of the old stuff that you don't want, you are literally creating physical space for the new things that bring beauty, meaning, and utility to your home. The message here is that it's okay to let go of the old baggage in order to make room for what you do want.

Decluttering may feel like a huge task, so I'll make it easy on you. Try spending twenty minutes a day on it. Start with cleaning out one drawer; every time you open that drawer you'll get a good feeling. Now, continue working in the same room till it's completely decluttered. Then move on to another room. Visualize your home six weeks from now. That should be a great incentive.

Restore Order When you think of restoring order to your living space, do you immediately think of your daughter's room, where her clothes, books, and homework are scattered all over the floor? It's tempting to focus on your daughter's chaos, but for now I want to focus on you.

Let's concentrate on two simple things that can help you organize the chaos: first, finding a place for everything in your home, and, second, getting things in working order. I know this information is not new to you, but if you've been really busy or constantly dealing with drama, your home can end up chaotic and disorganized by default.

1. **Find a place for everything.** You want to make sure that everything in your home has a place. This includes keys, cell phones, documents, magazines, reading glasses, staplers, books—everything! You know how much time your daughter wastes when she can't find her clothes for school or her dance shoes. But how much time do you waste when you can't find a writing pen that works? Make a list of things that you habitually search for, like your tweezers, and establish a place for them; walk through the house and make a list of everything that doesn't have a place.

2. **Get things in working order.** When things are in working order, your life runs smoothly. But when they aren't attended to, they can break down and cause extra time and frustration. Your daughter tries to print out her homework and there is no ink

in the printer. The dryer stops working and all your clothes are wet. Your coffee maker breaks down (a broken coffee maker can really get to you). Give your home and possessions some attention. Take twenty minutes and walk through the house with a pad and pencil. Make a list of everything that is not in working order. Then attend to one thing a day. The good news is that most of these items can be fixed in a short amount of time, and will end up saving you a great deal of time.

Get Rid of False Obligations

You can also clear your plate by getting rid of false obligations. An obligation is something that you feel you must do, although in reality you have a choice. False obligations can come from others or you can place them on yourself. When it's a false obligation, it's hard to say no because you will feel too guilty.

False obligations show up in the "shoulds" of your life:

- I *should* cook dinner every night of the week.

- I should be willing to drop everything every time my needy friend calls.

- I *should* volunteer at school.

- I *should* send out my holiday cards.

- I *should* be available for my boss/partner/daughter any time he or she needs me.

Getting rid of the false obligations in your life frees your time and energy for what's important to you and your family. Are there any "shoulds" in your life that prevent you from spending time on what you need or want to do?

Ask for Help

Finally, clear your plate by asking for help. This means letting go of feeling as if you have to do everything yourself. It means giving up some control and responsibility to someone else. It can be difficult for moms to delegate or ask for help. There are lots of reasons why we resist asking for help from others:

- **"It's my job. I should be able to do this on my own."** This is one more of those terrible "shoulds" you've been burdening yourself with. You can't do it all on your own without compromising your mental or physical health and your priorities.

- **"I don't have the money."** Asking for help doesn't have to cost you money. Many items on your plate can and should be handled by the members of your family. Ask them to give you a hand when you need it.

- **"I don't trust anyone else to get the job done."** It's easier for me to do it myself." This is a control issue. You need to go back to your Priority Pie and see the big picture. Does it *really* matter how the dishwasher is loaded or if the laundry's folded in a specific way? Get over it! To recapture the life you love, you need to compromise on the small things in order to focus on those most important to you.

- **"I'm already too busy. I don't have time to figure this out."** Take ten minutes and write down three things that you're tired of doing, and which member of the household should take on each of those tasks. Imagine how good it will feel when they are off your plate. A few minutes can save you a lot of time.

Then there are those times when there is too much to do and your family can't help you out. This doesn't mean that if they can't, you can and should. This is where resentment can creep in. If they can't and you can't, you need to ask for more help.

In the last chapter, we talked about building a team to support your daughter, and you can do the same. Where do you need extra help? Your team could include anyone and everyone, from a housekeeper, handyman, or personal assistant to a mentor, therapist, or personal trainer. You're worth every penny—and the entire family will reap the benefits of a happier, healthier you!

I had a mom once tell me that she felt like her daughter's personal assistant. "I wish I had my own personal assistant," she said. Actually she could, and you can too. Just think outside of the box. You can hire a college student for two hours a week. Even freeing up two hours a week can make a big difference in your life.

Schedule the Life You Want

Now that you've cleared your plate, it's time to schedule the life you want. You've already had ample experience overseeing complex family schedules, and you now know how to schedule activities in the second and third quadrant of the Power Pie. But now we need to add your important and energizing priorities to your schedule. I call this "scheduling your treasures."

But let's begin with two scheduling tips that will help you recapture the life you loved and get things done more efficiently.

Take Time to Plan

When you're busy, you may feel you don't have time to plan. However, you plan in other areas of your life. As the CEO of your own life you can book business meetings for yourself to plan the life you want now and in the future.

Here are four ways you can stay on track:

1. **Schedule a daily focus meeting.** Spend ten minutes each morning and identify one important thing you would like to accomplish that day.

2. **Schedule a Sunday start-up meeting.** This is your weekly planning meeting. Take thirty minutes and reflect on what you accomplished from the prior week. Set an intention for the upcoming week. Now identify your goals and priorities and turn them into action items. Make sure you write them down in your calendar.

3. **Schedule three "recapture your life" half-day meetings a year.** This is a time to write down everything you accomplished in the past four months. Use this long meeting (think of it as a company retreat) to reflect on "what's working," "what's not working," and "what I can do better." Revisit the Priority Pie, and make sure your priorities are in alignment with how you spend your time. Strategize ways you can reduce your workload by saying no, delegating, or hiring extra help. Set new goals and create new intentions for the next four months.

4. **Schedule a "plan for the future" meeting.** I often hear moms ask, "What will I do when my daughter graduates from high school." Schedule time *now* to think about what's next for you. Answer these questions. What would bring you joy and fulfillment? Is it time for a new career? What does your ideal future look like? Plan your future now and begin taking the necessary steps to make it a reality.

Manage Different Energies

Another way of thinking about scheduling your day is that you are managing different energies. Reflection and focused concentration require one kind of energy, and being social, playful, and engaging require another. In addition, your mental and physical energy ranges from optimal to depleted over the course of a single day. It's important to know the times your mind is more alert and clear and when you have peak physical energy. Knowing this will help you accomplish tasks more resourcefully. For example, there are certain times of the day where you may find yourself constantly interrupted. You want to plan activities for that time that won't be affected if you're disturbed. This is not the time to finish a report that needs your complete concentration. It's why you want to intentionally schedule alone (uninterrupted) time at some point during the day for activities that need your full attention. Do this by setting an alarm for an hour and turning off your phone.

There are also certain times of day when you have more clarity and energy. Schedule your activities accordingly. For example, I'm most clear-headed in the morning, so that's the best time for me to write. For some reason, I have more energy in the evening, so that's a better time to exercise.

Another way to manage your energies is by batching. For example, one day you create a menu for the week and go grocery shopping. The next day you do meal preparation for the week. This saves you from scrambling each night to make dinner. Are there any weekly tasks you can batch?

Schedule Your Treasures

To schedule your treasures, you need to know what your treasures are. You can find many of your treasures in the first quadrant of your Priority Pie. For instance, some of my treasures that make life worthwhile to me are:

- Hanging out with my daughter at the end of the day

- Having Sunday night dinner with my parents

- Riding my bike

- Taking time to meditate and pray

- Having a relaxed dinner with a good friend

- Making time to relax and putter in the house or yard

Now it's your turn. Write down all your treasures that are important and that energize you.

To recapture the life you love, you need to schedule your treasures first, before any of the items on your family to-do list. When you schedule your treasures, you are making a commitment to yourself (remember Powerful Parenting Message #2, "Commitment to yourself is the foundation for commitment to your family"?). You are taking yourself and your priorities seriously. You schedule your treasures like you would any other appointment. Then you honor that appointment and keep it.

Scheduling your treasures is very doable. You can start small. Pick one treasure that you'd like to schedule time for—whether it's reading a book, meditating, writing in your journal, walking around the block, or watching a video with your daughter—and then schedule that activity for fifteen minutes a day. You'll be amazed at how these fifteen minutes can energize you.

This has transformed my life. When I started scheduling my treasures, I became a better mom because I was more patient and more present to my daughter. I was also in a better mood, and a lot more fun to be around.

* * *

You don't have to wait till your daughter leaves home before you recapture the life you love. Start recapturing it today by getting clear about your priorities and getting them into your schedule. It's up to you to identify your priorities and schedule the life you want. Your treasures will replenish your mind, body, heart, and soul. The good news is that you don't have to be miserable during your daughter's teenage years. If you use these practical strategies you can begin enjoying the life you love today.

CHAPTER 12

How to Be Your Daughter's Dream Maker

Since she was four years old, my daughter's dream was to be a famous ballerina. She would wear what she called "pink turnarounds" and spin across the living room floor. From the time she was five until she was eleven she went to dance class once a week. When she was twelve, she went to a more serious dance studio and took classes at least four days a week, as well as private lessons from her instructor.

My daughter made significant progress, and decided to apply for a competitive dance program at a high school for performing arts. The school had a long list of former students and their many success stories. Every year graduating students were accepted to New York University, Julliard, and prestigious ballet companies, and many started their careers on Broadway. This only fueled my daughter's dream to be a dancer.

It seemed like forever, but finally the letter came. I'll never forget the joy on her face when she told me she had been accepted. For the next three years she lived the life of a dancer. I invested in private lessons. I was even a dorm mom at a summer dance intensive so my daughter could attend. I was very proud of her. Watching her dance brought me great joy. I did everything I could to support her. It was her dream, but it also became my dream for her too.

Then, in her junior year of high school, things started to unravel. I was slow to see that my daughter was getting tired of the pressure and competitive nature of dance. She could have pushed through that, but her body began to fail her. During the spring semester she suffered injuries to both of her knees, and had a major shoulder injury. At this point it was becoming apparent she needed to take a break. My daughter was clear that this was the right decision, but I really wrestled with it. Was my daughter quitting on her dream? I decided to let her change schools because she needed to let her body heal— and her heart and soul.

It turned out to be the best thing for her. After a knee operation and a summer of physical therapy, she started getting interested in art.

My daughter was fine; I was the one who needed to let go. I had to realize that there would not be just one dream, but *many* during her life.

Identifying Your Daughter's Dream

It's difficult to know what your daughter's dream is. It's rare that a girl knows who she wants to be when she grows up, and even if she does, it can change at any moment. This is really hard for moms. Patty's daughter, Madison, loved swimming, was an amazing swimmer, and talked about continuing swimming competitively after high school. But then, when she was actually offered a fully paid university scholarship for her swimming, she decided she was tired of the competition and quit the team her senior year—and gave up the scholarship. I've seen girls who excelled in ice skating, dancing, gymnastics, theatre, and band make similar choices in high school, despite their mothers' protests.

As a mom, it's hard to know what's the right thing to do. You can't help but be concerned that your daughter may later regret a decision to give up on what had been her dream. But do you push her to stay the course, or do you respect her decision? Sometimes, because you have invested your money, time, energy, and emotions, your daughter's dream can become more your dream than hers. To be able to identify her dream, you need to examine society's dream (the one you've been conditioned to expect your daughter to achieve), your personal dream for her, and her dream for herself.

The "Dream"

The "dream," as defined by our culture, tells us what a successful teenager should be looking for in her life. She makes good grades. She gets a good scholarship because of her academics and her other achievements. She's clear about her major and gets accepted to the university of her choice. She graduates in four years and may decide to continue her education. After college she finds a job quickly, one with a substantial salary. During this time she starts dating a wonderful man who has a promising future. There's a lot of pressure on both mom and daughter to achieve the dream society has dictated.

It's assumed that this dream is achieved in a smooth, straight path. When it's not, a mom can feel embarrassed, stressed, and even shamed about her daughter's future. The truth is, society's dream is simply another form of perfectionism. Your daughter's dream is not a straight, smooth path; it's more like a circuitous journey filled with challenges and detours. Accepting that there is not just one dream can take the pressure off you and your daughter. She can define the dream that's best for her. It's not just a trite saying; there really are many paths to success.

Your Dream for Your Daughter

What is your dream for your daughter? Take thirty minutes and write it out on a sheet of paper. What do you think she should do after she graduates from high school? Do you want her to go to college? What do you want her to major in?

Because you are so involved in your daughter's life, it can blind you to what is actually best for her—what meets her needs, her goals, and her desires. You may want her to experience what you enjoyed in college. Catherine was involved in a sorority in college and loved it. She wanted her daughter, Amy, to go to the state university and join the same sorority. Amy was more artsy, wanted to go to a small liberal arts college, and had no interest in being in a sorority. This caused a great deal of tension in their relationship. At first, Catherine thought her daughter was making the biggest mistake of her life. It wasn't until she had a long talk with Amy and understood that her daughter had given college a lot of thought that Catherine finally let go of her dream and supported Amy's dream. As it turned out, her daughter thrived in the liberal arts school.

If you have past regrets, you may push your daughter to achieve what you didn't. When Julie was graduated from high school, she went to a community college and lived at home. She later regretted that she didn't go away to college, where she would have more control over her life day to day. As a result, she pushed her daughter, Bianca, to apply for colleges out of state, but Bianca wanted to stay home and work for a year. Mom worried that Bianca only wanted to stay in town because she didn't want to leave her boyfriend, a year behind her in school. This was upsetting for mom, especially since Bianca had been accepted by an excellent university. Bianca told her mom that she didn't want to go to college until she had decided on a major. In the end, this was a good decision for Bianca. After working hard at a coffee shop for a year, Bianca knew what career path she wanted to take and was ready to go away to college.

Your Daughter's Dream for Herself

A year ago, a high school friend found me on Facebook. She messaged me saying, "Do you remember what your big goal was when we graduated?" I had no idea. "To date a long-haired guy," she said. I have no idea if that is really true, but it could have been. We've talked about the undeveloped teenage brain, and this was definitely true of mine at eighteen. I'm sure glad my dreams have evolved since then, and you can be sure that your daughter's will too.

It's hard when your daughter's dreams are different from yours and conflict with your values. Alesha is the mother of Nadia who is sixteen years old. Alesha came to see me because she wanted a better relationship with Nadia. She told me, "We used to be close, but it all changed one afternoon when I was taking her home from school. I had a lot on my mind, the radio was blaring, and we were stuck in traffic. This is when Nadia told me she liked girls and that she was gay. I was shocked. This goes against my religion. To be honest, I don't even remember what I said, but the message she got was that I didn't accept her."

She went on: "In the months that followed I tried to convince her that I would love her no matter what, but she didn't believe me. Since then she struggled with depression and kept her distance from me. Six months ago we both got into therapy and it's been helping. Last week out of the blue Nadia asked me with a smile on her face, 'Would you love me if I was a panda bear?' (My daughter loves pandas.) I kissed her on the forehead and rubbed her arm and told her, 'Of course I would.' That moment marked a real change for us."

Obviously this was a painful journey for both Alesha and Nadia. But in the end what really mattered was neither Nadia's sexual orientation, nor Alesha's initial feelings about it; what mattered was that Nadia finally came to believe again that her mom loved her, no matter what.

Regina was on the faculty of an Ivy League school. Her daughter wanted to drop out of high school and get her GED. Academics were difficult for her and she didn't feel like she belonged at her high school. She wanted to go to cosmetology school. Her dream was to be a hairdresser. Her mother wouldn't hear of it; she wanted her daughter to graduate high school and get a degree from a prestigious college. Her daughter was intimidated by her mom and felt she couldn't be truthful with her, so she finished high school and went to a community college, where she made D's and had to drop several classes that she was failing. Because this wasn't her dream, Regina wasn't invested in college, and this was reflected in her grades.

You may feel you're open-minded, but there's a good chance that your daughter's choices will rub against what you think is best for her. There are times you are right, but this deserves some real soul-searching. Is what you want for your daughter really about you, or what's best for your daughter? Are you embarrassed about what your daughter's dream is, or think it's not valid? This was the case with Regina; she didn't want her daughter going to a trade school. This definitely challenged society's dream for her daughter.

There are loads of girls who know exactly what they want, which is great, but there are also plenty who don't. What if your daughter doesn't know what her dream is and wants to take some time off to figure out what she wants? I have seen many college girls fail out their freshmen year. They definitely got an A+ in partying and dating but that's about all. They had no motivation to study because they were unclear about their major and weren't emotionally ready. Understandably, their parents were upset. These girls would have benefited from what is called a "gap year."

The gap year has become increasingly popular. According to the American Gap Association, a gap year is: "A structured period of time when students take a break from formal education to increase self-awareness, learn from different cultures, and experiment with possible careers. Typically, these are achieved by a combination of traveling, volunteering, interning, or working." One of the association's statistics stated, "Ninety percent of students who took a gap year returned to college within a year." There are many advantage of the gap year. It allows students to grow in maturity, clarity, independence, and confidence.

Society's dream for your daughter may not fit, because teenage girls have different interests, social needs, learning styles, and levels of maturity. But today, happily, there are more choices. Just like your specific preferred coffee drink, your daughter can design a dream that meets her specific tastes, personality, learning style, needs, and abilities.

Letting Go

Letting go of your teenage daughter is hard, but necessary. There are many upsides to letting go. You gradually let go so she can become more autonomous and independent. You let go of your dreams, so she can discover her own. You let go because she is taking on more responsibilities and is more emotionally mature. But what if she is not mature? What if she's not making good choices? This is the scary part of the teenage years. Once you let go, you don't know if she will walk tall or fall flat on her face. Yet, you still need to let go.

Letting go doesn't mean that you let go of guiding, protecting, or being invested in your daughter. It doesn't mean that you let go of your relationship with your daughter, but it does mean that you let go of control, and fear, and *your* dream.

Letting Go of Control

At some point during the teenage years you need to let go of trying to control your daughter. It may be hard to distinguish between what constitutes control and what is necessary to protect and guide her. Being controlling means that there is only one way, and it's your way. One reason for your need to control your daughter may be that you're trying to live your life through her. This doesn't work for either of you. She has the right to have her own life, as do you.

Letting go of control also means that you stop being Monitor Mom. You can't micromanage everything your daughter does without incurring her resentment. The more you try to control, the more she will push back. She will rebel directly and forcefully or be passive-aggressive and avoid you. In reality, you can't control who your daughter chooses as friends or who she falls in love with. You can't control her choices, thoughts, feelings, or what she believes. You can't control what your daughter will do when you're not around. The irony is that if you let go of the control, you have more influence in your daughter's life. She will stop resisting you and come to you freely with her problems. Then you can give her guidance.

Letting go of control doesn't mean that you're passive; in fact, it's the opposite. It takes a great deal of soul-searching to determine when you are being too controlling of your daughter's life, and when you need to let go.

Letting Go of Your Fear

Letting go of control is giving your daughter some space to grow up and discover who she is. This can be frightening. Fear fuels control. You may feel that if you let go of control, something horrible will happen and you'll lose your daughter forever. There are many unknowns about your daughter's future, and this can create fear in you. (This is a good time to review the section entitled Dismantle the F-Bomb on pages 39–43 of Chapter 2.) Working through your fear enables you to identify what you *do* need to do to protect your daughter.

Now that you've excavated the truth from your fear and taken action, you can let it go. Remove fear from the driver's seat, because it will drive you straight back to stress response. What helps you let go of fear is remembering that your fear is a thought created by your imagination. It's not reality. You don't want this scary movie playing over and over in your mind. Rewrite the script. What do you want to happen? Now play this movie in your imagination. If you're afraid your daughter won't get accepted into a well-known university, imagine her reading her acceptance letter to what will be the perfect college *for her.* It will not only bring you peace, but will change how you approach your daughter.

Letting Go of Your Dream

Your daughter has the right to have her own dream. You can't live vicariously through her. It's not her responsibility to live your dreams or heal your regrets.

My dad's dream for me was to get an MBA and make a good living. And what did I do? I spent seven years getting my BFA and MFA in painting, and didn't use my major to make a living. And I wouldn't change a thing. Later, I went back to graduate school and got my degrees in counseling (Dad wasn't crazy about that, either)—and here I am today, writing a book! Even though I don't have my MBA, my parent's are so proud of me because I'm living my dream—as you hope your daughter will live *hers!*

Motivating Your Teenage Daughter

You want your daughter to thrive. You feel successful when she is suc-cessful. But when you don't feel your daughter is on the right path, it creates anxiety and stress, and when you're stressed, it makes it very difficult to motivate her. This is when it's easy to slip into panicking, belittling, and making negative predictions, turning your own fear into a prediction of what you believe will happen to her. You end up becoming your daughter's *stress* maker instead of being her *dream* maker.

To truly motivate your daughter you need to decrease the pressure on her and avoid all negativity. You motivate by building on your daughter's strengths and being a thoughtful encourager. You invest in her dreams. You create positive experiences that instill curiosity and adventure. And you become a model to your daughter by being *your* own dream maker.

Decrease the Pressure

Over the past ten years, my office has been packed with anxious, stressed-out high school girls. These girls are so worried about their future success that it affects their academic performance. A little pressure is useful and can be motivating. Too much pressure is debilitating because it triggers the stress response (fight, flight, or freeze). This is why your daughter can freeze up on a test and not retain information when she studies. This may also be why your daughter procrastinates. She takes flight from what is causing her stress, which could be her chemistry test.

Decrease your daughter's stress by first decreasing your own. Only then can you reassure her. The greatest gift you can give your daughter is to be able to calm her stress and anxiety.

Avoid Negative Predictions

When your daughter is doing well, it's easy to encourage her. The challenge is when she is not studying, and is blowing off her responsibilities at home. This is when the sarcasm, shame, labeling, belittling, and negative predictions can begin. You think that if you scare your daughter with your predictions, she will do what's right. But negative predictions never motivate; they only damage your relationship with your daughter and damage her self-confidence.

I met with Cheryl once. She told me that she had been "losing it" with her eighteen-year-old daughter Kaylee. Cheryl was well dressed and soft-spoken, and it was hard for me to imagine her losing it. But the following week, when I saw Kaylee, she told me that she and her mom fought all the time. I listened to one of their fights, which she had recorded on her phone, and Cheryl was indeed out of control, screaming, "You'll never be successful. You won't get accepted to that university you want to go to, and if you do, I'm not paying for it."

Cheryl didn't mean what she said. She was fearful about her daughter's future and finances. But when she lost it, her fears would surface with these negative predictions, which would create terrible anxiety in her daughter, and contributed to Kaylee's poor self-esteem. It also ticked her off. She would strike back at mom, which would then increase her mother's panic. Nothing positive comes from negative predictions.

If you've made negative predictions in the past, it's important to repair the damage with your daughter. You do this by taking responsibility for your actions. Name the fear that prompted the negative prediction. Ask forgiveness for the words you said out of anger. And give her a positive prediction to replace the negative prediction like "I know you will be accepted to the right college for you."

Teenagers are enthusiastic about life and all the possibilities before them. You don't want to kill their optimism through negative predictions.

Build on Your Daughter's Strengths

Your daughter is motivated when she believes she has the ability and talent to achieve success. You can build her confidence by acknowledging her strengths and recognizing each accomplishment. During difficult times between you, it can be hard to keep her positive attributes in mind. This is when you need to take time to remember how amazing your daughter truly is.

Begin by recalling her strong points. Spend thirty minutes writing out all her character strengths, social skills, and abilities. Identify her unique features. If you can't think of anything positive about your daughter now, go back to her childhood.

Next, identify her *hidden* strengths in what frustrates you. Your daughter may blow off her homework because she wants to hang out with her friends. The hidden strength is that she has good people skills and might be good at networking. These social abilities can be very useful in her career. If your daughter is strong-headed and likes to argue, she may make a great lawyer. Identifying her hidden strengths can build her confidence and calm you down in the process.

Lastly, you want your daughter to know that you believe in her, even in the most challenging times. Be a thoughtful encourager (reread Chapter 10) on a consistent basis. Notice the small increments of positive change. Like most of us, your daughter may not see she's making improvement. Because her teenage brain tends to see things in extremes, she thinks that she's the worse person on the team or the fattest person in her class or the stupidest person in the whole school. Point out where you see her making progress. It doesn't matter how small the change, let her know she's moving forward. This gives her the hope she needs to stay the course.

Be Invested

Be your daughter's dream maker by investing in her dreams. She knows you take her talents seriously when you invest your money, time, and energy. When I was a little girl, my parents would buy me art supplies whenever I asked and would regularly compliment my drawings and paintings. These actions motivated me to pursue my talent.

Also, invest in your relationship with your daughter by keeping on top of what she's interested in and how she's doing. Invest by soothing her when she experiences setbacks or failure. Invest by redirecting her when she gets off course, and tenaciously be her thoughtful encourager.

A surprising way you can invest in your daughter's dream is to invest in your own. When you invest in your own dreams you model to your daughter what's possible for her. If she sees you take risks, fail, start over, and ultimately achieve success, she will identify with you and believe the same is possible for her as well.

Facilitate Positive Experiences

Another way you motivate your daughter is by providing positive experiences. These experiences instill curiosity and give her positive adventures.

Instill Curiosity For your daughter to be a lifelong learner, she needs to access her own curiosity. Telling a teen to memorize or read a chapter because she needs to make good grades will only get her so far. Grades are motivating, but the real reward is satisfying her curiosity. There are times you need to pressure her to study; but ultimately you want to instill in her a curiosity to learn. This gives her an internal motivation to pursue her interests. Give her opportunities for experiential learning, like going to the ocean for her marine biology class.

You can also model being curious to your daughter. I tend to be a brain geek, and would talk to my daughter about all the cool things I was learning about the brain. She would say, "OMG, Mom, enough about the brain." But a year later she was reading her own books about the brain (books that she bought unbeknownst to me) and now she shared her cool brain facts with *me.*

When your daughter discovers her own curiosity, she is well on her way to discovering her dreams.

Promote Positive Adventures A high school senior recently told me that she was bored, depressed, and that there was nothing new in her life. Teens can get depressed if they are not getting enough stimulation.

Your daughter is hard-wired for a real live adventure, not a digital one. An adventure is a new exciting experience when it includes curiosity, learning, challenges and an element of risk. This is fueled by the drive for the dopamine reward that I discussed in Chapter 7. If you don't provide positive, adult-approved opportunities for adventure, your daughter will create them. She'll create an adventure one way or another, because teens hate to be bored. The adventure she creates could be dangerous because of her taking *big* impulsive risks. Give your daughter positive adventures like travel (the more exotic the better, but anywhere new will do); encourage her to engage in adventure sports like snowboarding, backpacking, or rock-climbing.

Redefining What It Means to Be a Successful Teen

It's time to redefine what it means to be a successful teenage girl. It's more than being the most popular girl at school or its valedictorian or star athlete. It goes much deeper than that. Your daughter is a successful teenage girl when . . .

- She learns from her mistakes.

- She fails but keeps trying.

- She enjoys her sports and activities regardless of how she performs.

- She shows compassion and kindness to others.

- She works hard and shows improvement.

- She takes the road that's right for her.

Now there's a daughter to be proud of!

When you redefine the "successful teenage girl," it takes the pressure off of you and your daughter because it's not about being perfect. You're not devastated when there are interruptions and obstructions. You know that setbacks can develop her character and maturity. Because you know that society's dream doesn't fit all teens, you feel comfortable as she moves into a future that matches her uniqueness.

Expect Interruptions and Obstructions

You think your daughter is on her right path and then the interruption happens. Seventeen-year-old Shelby was a junior in a private high school. She made mostly A's, was active in the drama club, and had a beautiful singing voice. She had the lead in the high school musical. Right before the winter break, she was diagnosed with mononucleosis. It hit her hard. She not only missed her finals, but she was home for the next three months and had to give up her lead role in the musical. In April, Shelby started to go back to school part-time, which was hard for her. She felt that her friends had moved on. She worried that she couldn't catch up on her class work. This was extremely painful for her mom. Mom was also worried about how this would impact Shelby's future. However, Shelby tapped into her inner resilience. The mononucleosis was an *interruption* but didn't stop Shelby. She was able to get back on track with her grades, and friends before the spring semester had ended.

Life brings interruptions as well as the obstructions that your daughter brings on herself. How do you handle obstructions like when your daughter gets pregnant, fails a class, totals the car, gets fired from her job, gets caught with drugs, or gets arrested for a DWI? How do you handle your daughter when she is in a difficult emotional place? When you discover she is bulimic or anorexic? When she gets severely depressed after breaking up with her first real boyfriend?

How you handle these moments matters a lot. Of course you don't want these things to happen, but when they do, will you stand beside her? This is when she needs you the most. She needs you to hold the hope for her until she gets back on her feet. She needs your unconditional love, forgiveness, grace, and support. More than ever, she needs you to believe in her.

Define the "Best Next Step"

To redefine what it means to be "a successful teenage girl," you must determine what the "best next step" is for your daughter. This is an important question for both you and your daughter. The best next step is the one that helps your daughter grow in responsibility, emotional maturity, confidence, clarity, knowledge, and skill. It sets your daughter up for success and builds confidence, even though it may look different from society's dream for her.

The best next step starts with where your daughter is emotionally and developmentally. If your daughter is not emotionally healthy, then taking care of her issues is the best next step. Sheila's daughter was in a tumultuous relationship with her boyfriend. She was depressed and would put herself at risk by driving drunk. Her mother would receive texts like, "I'm going to drive my car into a tree. No one loves me." Three weeks later, her daughter left for college. The old issues followed her and the mother still got the desperate texts, but now her daughter was five hours away. It would have been much better for them both if she had tackled those issues before she left for college.

Once you assess where your daughter is, you define the best next step. This is all about the right timing. Some girls have their bags packed by the spring semester of their senior year of high school. They are ready to go to college, and that's wonderful. That's the best next step. But if it's not right for your daughter, there are options. The best next step allows your daughter to grow in confidence and maturity. Identifying the best next step comes from truly listening to your daughter and paying attention to her wants and needs. If she wants to take a gap year, work full-time, take a semester off, go to cosmetology school, or become an apprentice chef, electrician, or plumber— that might be the best next step for her. The thing to remember is that once she has completed *this* best next step, she can take the *next* best next step. Each step takes her closer to her dreams.

* * *

Being your daughter's dream maker is quite a journey—one that is frustrating, fun, scary, rewarding, and joyful.

You must avoid imposing society's dream or your own dream (for yourself or for her) on her, and together, the two of you must determine her best next step.

The hard part of being your daughter's dream maker is letting go, but there's a giant payoff. You're able to watch her life unfold as she discovers her unique gifts and callings. Your dreams for her may be good, but her dreams can far surpass all that you hoped for.

CHAPTER 13

Why You Need a Long-Term Perspective

A while back, I was speaking to a local organization of mothers of teenage daughters. At the end of my talk, five sophisticated, well-dressed moms came up to me and told me I had been their youth leader when they were in high school. Prior to becoming a therapist, I had spent ten years as a youth minister and had hung out with teens in all kinds of situations, from high school lunches to football games. I hadn't seen any of these women since the late 1980s, and, wow, they had changed. However, I still remembered all the crazy stuff they had done in their teen years. Once, on a weekend trip with two vans full of girls, the girls in my van were throwing tampons at the other van as I was driving sixty-five miles an hour down the freeway. Besides these kinds of pranks, I knew their secrets. I knew what boys they had sex with. I knew when they got drunk or smoked weed, or stole their parents' credit cards, or snuck out at night. Yet all of these women turned into responsible adults and now had their own teenage daughters.

I think as moms we forget that we were teenagers once, and that we did a lot of crazy stuff too. Despite our little secrets and mistakes, we made it safely to adulthood, and your daughter will as well. When raising a teenage girl, it helps to have a long-term perspective. In high school I gave my mom several grey hairs, but in college we worked through our issues and started spending time together. We've since had almost forty years of a close, authentic and enjoyable relationship.

A long-term perspective brings you comfort and hope during your daughter's teenage years. It puts your frustrations and fears into the proper context when you remember where your daughter is developmentally and why she's hard-wired for drama. It also helps you see the positive attributes of a teenage girl and how that girl can bring you joy and enhance your life.

A long-term perspective also reminds you that there's life beyond the teenage years. Your daughter will become an adult, and you'll have many more years and experiences to share together. Remembering this will help motivate you to protect your connection with your daughter in high school and not cause irreparable damage, because you want to have a healthy relationship that lasts a lifetime.

A Healthy Perspective on Your Daughter's Teenage Years

It's easy to lose a healthy perspective when you are worried, frustrated, angry, or saddened by your daughter's choices and actions. To have a healthy perspective, you need to take a step back and look at your daughter's teenage years as just one chapter in a much longer story. Fundamental to this perspective is keeping in mind that your daughter is a work in progress. On the other side of all the drama are many positive attributes and qualities. Teens are hilarious, adventurous, and fun to be around. Your teenage daughter can not only enhance your life but she can remind you what it means to live a rich and vibrant life.

Remember That Your Daughter Is a Work in Progress

What make the teenage years challenging is your daughter's impulsivity, risk taking, and tendency not to think things through, or process cause and effect. It can also be frustrating dealing with your drama princess, with her volatile mood swings and her melodramatic reactions. Much of these irritations are because your daughter's brain is under reconstruction and is being remodeled, which I discussed in Chapter 7. As she matures, most of these annoyances and concerns will fade away.

Many moms make the mistake of equating their daughter's immature thinking and actions with her personality. This is really more about her undeveloped brain than who she truly is. Her personality, her essence, gets hidden under all of her lower brain reactions. When your daughter is not in stress response, you can catch glimpses of her emerging personality, and her beautiful essence will continue to unfold as she matures into adulthood.

Everything in this book has been intended to help you keep things in perspective so you can enjoy your daughter's teenage years. Now let's look at the upside of the teenage years and how this can bless and benefit you.

What's Good About Teens

I love being around teenagers. They have an energy and joy that's contagious. When you can get past the drama, you can see their wonderful attributes and qualities, many of which we lose as adults.

Yes, teens can be emotionally reactive, but they can also be emotionally alive. They laugh and play hard. When they are not stressed, they are carefree and living in the present. The simplest of things bring them joy. They know how to have fun and enjoy their life. They have crushes and fall deeply in love. They are excited about what they like to do. Teens have a spark and vibrancy that many adults have lost. If your daughter is going to her favorite concert, she could literally be jumping up and down with excitement. In contrast, if you are going to a concert you might not feel anything at all. I'm not saying that we should be jumping up and down, but we should feel something positive. Your daughter can remind you that life is meant to be lively and fully charged.

Teens hate to be bored, and that's not a bad thing. They won't accept that being bored is an option, so they'll do something about it.

They will go on a quest for new and fun experiences. One of the things I love about my daughter is that she gets me out of my boring routine. She's constantly introducing me to new kinds of music, instead of me listening to my Golden Oldies from the 1970s and 1980s. She gets me out of my restaurant ruts, by having us go downtown and trying different kind of foods.

Teens have a fresh take on life. They question and don't accept the status quo. They feel deeply about the problems in the world. They aren't numb to issues like world hunger, or what we are doing to our environment. They question why there is war and what our government is doing. They are passionate and definitely have their opinions. Teens have much to offer adults because they have creative solutions and can think outside the box. They offer us new insights and can be extremely innovative. Adults tend to accept the status quo and can become indifferent to the injustices of the world, because we can become immersed in our own problems and responsibilities. Teens offer us a fresh perspective and can wake us out of our apathy.

Teens don't stay where they are; they continue to broaden their horizons. This could be traveling to new places or going off to college, but there's more to it than that. Expanding your horizons means stepping out of your comfort zone, and teens are continually doing this. They are meeting new people, learning new skills, and are constantly being challenged. Their world is continually expanding.

But it's different for moms. We can get very used to the way things are. It can be a little scary and uncomfortable to get out of our comfort zone. The problem is, if our world is not expanding, it's is shrinking. We're hanging out with the same old people, doing the same old thing. Our teens remind us that it is important to put ourselves out there, and keep growing. When you push past the discomfort, you feel exhilarated and alive. There is a satisfaction and delight that comes from meeting new people, traveling new places, and learning new skills. This brings us back to the importance of the personal enrichment needs that we discussed at length in Chapter 1 and then more briefly in Chapter 5. Expand your horizons by joining a networking group or book club, learning how to start a blog, or getting a certification for work—or how about, sailing around the world.

A Long-Term Perspective on Your Relationship with Your Daughter

A long-term perspective allows you to get through the teenage years with your relationship with your daughter intact. The information in this book empowers you to feel your best, which enables you to control your emotional reactions. Dialing down the drama is also dialing down the potential to do harm to you and your daughter. You don't want a strained and conflictual relationship to continue into the adult years. That's why you want to start building a satisfying relationship with your daughter now that will last a lifetime.

First Do No Harm

The Hippocratic oath that is used by physicians is "First do no harm." This is a good motto for both moms and daughters in the teenage years. You don't want to do harm to your daughter, of course, and you don't want her to do harm to you. Negative tactics of shame, labeling, belittling, controlling, yelling, threatening, and making negative predictions do harm to your daughter. It doesn't matter if you think you're doing it for a good reason. Using harmful methods as parenting tools will not have a good outcome. It will damage your relationship with your daughter, create stress, and cause her to avoid you. I have met with countless girls who, due to a tumultuous relationship with their moms, are counting the days till they graduate (and the moms are probably doing the same). They tell me they don't ever plan on coming home.

If you feel you have damaged your relationship with your daughter, it's not too late. Teens are pretty forgiving when you are loving, honest, and authentic. I know you can mend your relationship with your daughter, because I know you are committed. After all, you have read this book all the way to the end—which shows you care a great deal about your daughter. In this book I believe I have given you the tools you need to mend the relationship.

Create the Relationship You Want Now

A long-term perspective helps you reclaim the gratitude you felt when you first discovered you were pregnant with a baby girl. You want to hold on to that gratitude throughout her life. I have sat with moms who have lost their daughters in horrible car accidents. They would have done anything to have their daughters back, even with all their drama. It really is an amazing privilege and blessing to witness the un-folding of your daughter's personality, gifts, talents, and heart as she moves towards adulthood.

By now you understand that there is more to your relationship with your daughter than being the "heavy" and Monitor Mom, and you are learning how to avoid being a Drama Mama. You are also building a relationship that will take you both into her adult years. The elements that you build into your relationship now will be there twenty and thirty and forty years from now. You want to build a rela-tionship that is respectful, authentic, enriching, and enjoyable. These elements will help you get through the difficult parts of your relation-ship, especially when you have to pull out the mom card.

Let me repeat myself: It's not too late to rebuild a relationship with your teenage daughter. I see it in my counseling work over and over, and I've seen it in my own life. My daughter and I have definitely had our challenging moments—*extremely* challenging moments, believe you me—but now we truly enjoy being with each other. We both love animals, and enjoy live music. We are both creative and enjoy art, dance, and playing guitar. She will send me articles to read and shares interesting or amusing links that I enjoy reading. I love her enthusiasm for life and her sense of humor. These aspects of our relationship will keep us close and connected even after she leaves home.

What do you want your relationship with your daughter to be like in ten years? What interests do you share? What would you both enjoy doing? Start building this relationship now!

Index